BEFORE YOU VISIT TOKYO
(Travel Guide)

Insider Tips on Food, Fun, and Activities You
Don't Want to Miss

Joey A. Wolf

Disclaimer
This travel guide is designed to provide helpful information and insights for visitors to Tokyo. While every effort has been made to ensure accuracy, the author and publisher make no representations or warranties of any kind, express or implied, regarding the completeness, accuracy, reliability, suitability, or availability of the information contained in this book for any purpose. Readers are encouraged to verify information such as opening hours, prices, and transportation details, as these may change without notice.

The author and publisher shall not be held liable for any loss or damage, including indirect or consequential loss, arising from or in connection with the use of this guide. All travel is subject to potential risks, and travelers should exercise caution and make informed decisions according to their own personal and health needs. Additionally, any mention of specific companies, products, or services does not constitute endorsement or guarantee.

TABLE OF CONTENTS

INTRODUCTION

Tokyo is a city that stirs the imagination and captures the heart. As you prepare for your trip, you might already feel a sense of wonder about what awaits you. This is a place where ancient traditions live side by side with cutting-edge technology, and every street corner offers a new surprise. The city is alive with energy and possibility, but it also holds pockets of peace and quiet where you can catch your breath and take it all in. Tokyo is a city of contrasts, and these contrasts are part of what makes it so captivating. It is modern yet steeped in history, bustling yet serene, global yet deeply connected to its roots.

When you arrive in Tokyo, you'll notice how seamlessly the city blends old and new. Towering skyscrapers shimmer in the sunlight, their glass facades reflecting a vision of the future, while down a narrow alley, you might find a small temple that has stood for centuries. This coexistence is one of the first things that will strike you. It feels as though Tokyo is constantly moving forward, yet it never forgets its past. This balance creates an atmosphere that feels both exciting and comforting, as if the city is welcoming you to discover its many layers.

You might already have a picture in your mind of Tokyo's famous neon-lit streets, crowded crossings, and sleek bullet trains. While these images are true, they are just the beginning of what the city has to offer. Tokyo is not just one city; it's a collection of neighborhoods, each with its own character and charm. Some are filled with the buzz of people shopping, dining, and enjoying nightlife, while others are quieter, inviting you to slow down and enjoy a moment of reflection. The variety within Tokyo means there's always something new to experience, no matter what interests you.

One of the most striking things about Tokyo is its attention to detail. Whether you're walking through a park, exploring a traditional tea house, or even waiting for a train, you'll notice how much care has been taken to make things beautiful and efficient. Streets are impeccably clean, gardens are meticulously maintained, and every interaction feels thoughtful. This attention to detail extends to the way Tokyoites approach their daily lives, and it's something you'll come to appreciate during your stay. It makes even the smallest experiences like buying a snack from a convenience store or ordering coffee feel special.

Tokyo is also a city of endless flavors. Food is a way of life here, and you'll have the chance to try everything from sushi prepared by master chefs to street food served hot and fresh. The variety is astounding, and each meal feels like an adventure. You'll discover how the Japanese approach food with care and precision, whether it's a simple bowl of noodles or an elaborate multi-course meal. Eating in Tokyo isn't just about satisfying your hunger; it's about savoring the moment and connecting with the culture.

As you move through Tokyo, you'll also notice the rhythm of the city. It's fast-paced but not overwhelming, thanks to the way everything seems to work so smoothly. Trains arrive exactly on time, people move with purpose, and there's a sense of order that makes navigating such a large city feel surprisingly easy. At the same time, Tokyo encourages you to find your own rhythm. You can immerse yourself in the bustling streets of Shibuya or take a quiet walk through a garden in the early morning light. The city gives you the freedom to experience it however you choose.

There's also a deep respect for tradition that you'll feel throughout Tokyo. You might see it in a tea ceremony, where every movement is deliberate and meaningful, or in a festival where locals dress in traditional attire to celebrate their heritage. This respect for the past adds a richness to the city that you won't find in many other places. It's a reminder that while Tokyo is always looking ahead, it stays rooted in the customs and values that have shaped it for centuries.

This travel guide is here to help you make the most of your time in Tokyo. Whether you're interested in exploring its history, enjoying its modern attractions, or simply soaking up its unique atmosphere, you'll find all the information you need to plan an unforgettable trip. Tokyo is a place where every moment feels full of possibility, and we hope this guide will inspire you to experience the city to its fullest.

THE HISTORY OF TOKYO

Tokyo's history is as fascinating as the city itself, stretching back centuries to a time long before it became the vibrant metropolis you see today. When you visit Tokyo, you are stepping into a place that has evolved through eras of remarkable change. It began as a small fishing village known as Edo, situated along a peaceful river. In those early days, Edo was far from the bustling hub it is now, but its strategic location soon drew attention. By the 12th century, it had grown into a modest settlement, quietly thriving under local rule.

Everything changed in 1603 when Tokugawa Ieyasu, a powerful shogun, established Edo as the center of his government. This marked the start of the Edo period, a time when the city became the political and cultural heart of Japan. Under the Tokugawa shogunate, Edo flourished, transforming into a bustling city with a growing population. By the 18th century, it was one of the largest cities in the world. This era also saw the development of much of the culture and traditions that still influence Tokyo today, from kabuki theater to ukiyo-e woodblock prints.

The Edo period was a time of peace and strict order, but it came to an end in 1868 with the fall of the shogunate and the beginning of the Meiji Restoration. This was a pivotal moment in Tokyo's history. The emperor moved from Kyoto to Edo, renaming the city Tokyo, which means "Eastern Capital." It was during this time that Japan opened up to the world after centuries of isolation. Tokyo rapidly modernized, adopting

Western technology, architecture, and systems while still holding onto its cultural identity. You can imagine how dynamic this period must have been, with new railways, schools, and industries reshaping the city.

The 20th century brought both incredible growth and devastating challenges. Tokyo faced major disasters, including the Great Kanto Earthquake in 1923, which destroyed much of the city, and the firebombing during World War II, which left large parts of Tokyo in ruins. But each time, the city rebuilt itself with resilience and determination. After the war, Tokyo underwent a period of rapid reconstruction and modernization, laying the foundation for the global city it is today.

One of the key moments in Tokyo's modern history was the 1964 Summer Olympics. Hosting the Olympics marked Tokyo's return to the international stage, showcasing its recovery and newfound confidence. The event also led to significant developments, including new infrastructure and transportation systems that continue to serve the city. Since then, Tokyo has grown into one of the world's most influential cities, known for its innovation, culture, and hospitality.

What makes Tokyo's history so special is how it has managed to preserve its traditions while embracing the future. As you explore the city, you'll see remnants of its past woven seamlessly into the urban landscape. Historic temples and shrines stand proudly amidst sleek skyscrapers, and centuries-old festivals are celebrated with the same enthusiasm as ever.

This blend of old and new is a testament to Tokyo's unique ability to honor its roots while moving forward.

Understanding Tokyo's history gives you a deeper appreciation of the city's character. It's not just a collection of buildings or a hub of activity; it's a place shaped by centuries of transformation, resilience, and creativity. As you walk through its streets, you're not just exploring a modern capital\u2014you're connecting with a rich and remarkable past that continues to influence everything Tokyo is today.

WHY YOU SHOULD VISIT TOKYO

Imagine a city where every moment feels like an adventure. Tokyo is a place that captivates you with its energy, surprises you with its beauty, and leaves you with memories you'll cherish forever. As a tourist, you'll find yourself in a destination like no other, where the old and the new blend effortlessly, creating an experience that is both exciting and deeply enriching. From its towering skyscrapers to its peaceful gardens, Tokyo offers something for everyone, no matter what you're looking for.

As you explore Tokyo, you'll be struck by its diversity. One moment, you're standing in the middle of the famous Shibuya Crossing, surrounded by a sea of people and flashing lights, and the next, you're walking through the quiet grounds of a centuries-old shrine, feeling the calm wash over you. This contrast is what makes Tokyo so special. It's a city that can energize you with its modern marvels and soothe you with its timeless traditions, all within the same day.

For history lovers, Tokyo is a treasure trove of stories. You can feel the echoes of the past as you wander through its ancient temples and historic districts. The city has a way of making history come alive, with places that tell the tale of its journey from a small fishing village to the bustling capital of Japan. Even as you marvel at the city's modern skyline, you'll see reminders of its rich heritage in the details of its architecture, the rituals of its people, and the festivals that have been celebrated for generations.

If you're drawn to nature, Tokyo will surprise you with its peaceful green spaces. In the midst of the city's urban vibrancy, you'll find tranquil gardens, cherry blossoms that paint the streets in spring, and riverside paths where you can enjoy a quiet moment away from the hustle and bustle. Tokyo's connection to nature is a reminder of how deeply rooted Japanese culture is in the natural world, and it's a part of the city that you'll find refreshing and inspiring.

For food enthusiasts, Tokyo is a paradise. You'll be amazed by the variety and quality of the cuisine here, from exquisite sushi and savory ramen to creative street food and delicate sweets. Every meal in Tokyo feels like a celebration of flavor and craftsmanship. Whether you're dining at a Michelin-starred restaurant or grabbing a quick bite at a neighborhood eatery, you'll taste the care and passion that goes into every dish. Tokyo's food scene is more than a reason to visit; it's an experience you'll remember long after you've left.

Entertainment in Tokyo is like nowhere else. Whether you're exploring vibrant shopping districts filled with the latest trends, visiting quirky themed cafes, or enjoying traditional performances, there's always something new and exciting to discover. The city is alive with creativity, from its futuristic architecture to its cutting-edge art and design. You'll find inspiration at every turn, and no matter how much time you spend here, there will always be more to see and do.

Tokyo is also a place where you can relax and recharge. In addition to its buzzing streets and lively attractions, the city offers countless ways to unwind. Imagine soaking in a soothing hot spring bath, taking a peaceful stroll along a cherry tree-lined path, or sipping matcha tea in a serene teahouse. Tokyo has a way of making you feel both energized and at peace, and you'll leave with a sense of balance and renewal.

What sets Tokyo apart is its unique ability to offer something for everyone. It's a city that welcomes you with open arms and invites you to experience it in your own way. Whether you're an adventurer, a foodie, a history buff, or someone simply looking for a memorable getaway, Tokyo has something extraordinary waiting for you. It's not just a place to visit; it's a destination to fall in love with. And as you prepare to explore this incredible city, you'll discover that Tokyo isn't just a trip It's an unforgettable journey.

CHAPTER 1

PLANNING FOR YOUR TRIP

THE BEST TIME TO VISIT

When you plan your trip to Tokyo, the timing can shape your experience in the most delightful ways. Each season in Tokyo has its own charm, offering unique sights, activities, and a rhythm that changes with the weather. From the soft blush of cherry blossoms in spring to the crisp air of winter, Tokyo transforms throughout the year, ensuring there's always something special to discover no matter when you visit.

Spring in Tokyo, from March to May, is perhaps the most iconic time to visit. As the cold of winter gives way to warmer days, the city bursts into bloom with cherry blossoms, or sakura, creating a scene so beautiful it feels almost magical. You'll find locals and visitors alike gathering in parks like Ueno and Shinjuku Gyoen to enjoy hanami, or flower viewing, under canopies of pink and white. The weather during spring is mild and pleasant, with temperatures ranging from around 10 to 20 degrees Celsius (50 to 68 degrees Fahrenheit), making it an ideal time to explore Tokyo's gardens, temples, and outdoor attractions. This season also brings traditional festivals, such as the Kanda Matsuri, where vibrant processions fill the streets with music, color, and joy.

As summer arrives, Tokyo takes on a lively and energetic vibe. From June to August, temperatures rise to between 25 and 35 degrees Celsius (77 to 95 degrees Fahrenheit), and the city buzzes with activity. While the early part of summer brings the rainy season, with brief but intense showers, the skies often clear to reveal bright, sunny days perfect for summer festivals. You can experience events like the Sumida River Fireworks Festival, where dazzling displays light up the night, or the energetic dancing of the Awa Odori festival. Street markets and night stalls add to the festive atmosphere, offering seasonal treats like kakigori, a shaved ice dessert that's perfect for cooling down. Despite the heat, summer in Tokyo is unforgettable, filled with excitement and opportunities to immerse yourself in local traditions.

Fall, from September to November, is a season of golden light and cool, comfortable weather. With temperatures ranging from 15 to 25 degrees Celsius (59 to 77 degrees Fahrenheit), it's a wonderful time to explore Tokyo on foot, wandering through neighborhoods and parks that come alive with autumn colors. The foliage turns brilliant shades of red, orange, and yellow, creating picturesque scenes in places like Meiji Shrine's forested grounds or the gardens of Rikugien. Autumn also marks the harvest season, and you'll find seasonal foods like roasted chestnuts, sweet potatoes, and matsutake mushrooms being enjoyed across the city. Cultural festivals, including the annual Tokyo Ramen Show, celebrate the flavors of fall, offering a chance to sample a variety of ramen styles from across Japan.

Winter in Tokyo, from December to February, has its own quiet beauty. The city sparkles with illuminations, as streets and parks are decorated with millions of twinkling lights. Temperatures during winter range from 2 to 10 degrees Celsius (36 to 50 degrees Fahrenheit), and while snow is rare, the crisp, clear skies provide stunning views of Mount Fuji from observation decks or even certain city streets. Winter is a great time to visit Tokyo's hot springs, known as onsen, or enjoy warm, comforting dishes like oden, a traditional hotpot. The New Year period brings special traditions, such as hatsumode, the first shrine visit of the year, where you can witness locals praying for good fortune. It's also a quieter time for tourists, making it perfect for those who prefer a more relaxed atmosphere.

Ultimately, the best time to visit Tokyo depends on what you want to experience. If you're drawn to cherry blossoms and gentle breezes, spring is ideal. For vibrant festivals and summer energy, choose the warmer months. Autumn offers breathtaking scenery and perfect walking weather, while winter provides a magical, festive charm. No matter when you choose to go, Tokyo promises to enchant you with its ever-changing beauty and endless surprises, ensuring your visit is one to remember.

Packing Guidelines for Visiting Tokyo

Packing for a trip to Tokyo can feel like a challenge because the city offers so much to see and do, and its weather varies greatly depending on the season. With a little preparation, you can ensure you're ready for anything Tokyo has to offer. The key is to pack thoughtfully, considering both the time of year and the activities you plan to enjoy while you're there. Whether you're exploring ancient temples, strolling through vibrant neighborhoods, or savoring the city's culinary delights, having the right items in your suitcase will make your trip more comfortable and enjoyable.

If you're visiting Tokyo in spring, which lasts from March to May, you'll want to pack for mild and pleasant weather. Daytime temperatures usually range between 10 and 20 degrees Celsius (50 to 68 degrees Fahrenheit), so layering is essential. Light sweaters, cardigans, or jackets are perfect for staying comfortable as the temperatures fluctuate throughout the day. Don't forget a compact umbrella or a lightweight rain jacket, as occasional spring showers are common. Comfortable walking shoes are a must, especially if you plan to wander through Tokyo's parks and gardens to enjoy the cherry blossoms. Opt for footwear that can handle a mix of paved streets and natural trails, as some areas can be uneven.

Summer in Tokyo, from June to August, is hot and humid, with temperatures often reaching 30 to 35 degrees Celsius (86 to 95 degrees Fahrenheit). This season calls for light, breathable fabrics such as cotton or linen to help you stay cool. Short-sleeved tops, loose-fitting pants or skirts, and comfortable sandals are ideal for the heat. Since summer also brings the rainy season in June and early July, a compact, foldable umbrella or a lightweight waterproof jacket will come in handy. Sunscreen, a wide-brimmed hat, and sunglasses are essential to protect yourself from the strong sun. Don't forget to pack a reusable water bottle, as staying hydrated in the summer heat is crucial. If you plan to attend summer festivals or fireworks displays, consider bringing a small portable fan to keep cool and a casual yukata (a traditional cotton robe) if you want to blend in with the locals.

Autumn, which spans September to November, offers mild temperatures and stunning fall foliage. You'll need clothing that can adapt to a range of temperatures, as it's typically warm in early autumn and cooler by November. A mix of long-sleeved shirts, lightweight sweaters, and a mid-weight jacket will keep you comfortable. This is a wonderful season for exploring Tokyo on foot, so pack sturdy, comfortable shoes that can handle long days of walking. Layers are particularly helpful, as mornings and evenings can be cool while afternoons remain warm. If you're visiting parks or gardens to admire the fall colors, bring a small picnic blanket or a scarf to sit on while you relax outdoors.

Winter in Tokyo, from December to February, is generally cold but not harsh, with temperatures ranging from 2 to 10 degrees Celsius (36 to 50 degrees Fahrenheit). A warm coat, a scarf, gloves, and a hat are essential to stay cozy, especially if you're spending time outside visiting temples or shopping at outdoor markets. While snow is rare in the city, it's still wise to pack weatherproof boots or shoes with good traction, as some streets can be slippery in the early morning frost. Layering is key for winter visits, as indoor spaces like shops and restaurants are well-heated. Thermal underlayers, sweaters, and thick socks will keep you warm while exploring the city. If you plan to visit nearby mountains or hot springs, pack a swimsuit for onsen (hot spring) baths and extra warm clothing for colder temperatures in rural areas.

No matter the season, there are a few essentials that will make your trip to Tokyo more comfortable. A lightweight daypack or tote bag is perfect for carrying daily necessities like water, snacks, and souvenirs. Tokyo's streets are clean and well-kept, so a portable trash bag can help you dispose of waste responsibly when public bins are scarce. Bring a universal power adapter for charging your electronics, as Japan uses Type A and B plugs with a standard voltage of 100V. A reusable shopping bag is also helpful, as many stores in Tokyo charge for plastic bags. For sightseeing, a travel guidebook, map, or translation app can make navigating the city easier, especially if you're exploring more traditional areas where English signage is less common.

Tokyo's combination of modern conveniences and cultural traditions means that you may find yourself transitioning from casual activities to more formal occasions. To be prepared, consider packing at least one versatile outfit that can work for a nice dinner or an event like a tea ceremony. A smart-casual look, such as a collared shirt with slacks or a simple dress with comfortable flats, is usually appropriate. Additionally, if you plan to visit temples or shrines, bring modest clothing that covers your shoulders and knees to show respect for the sacred spaces.

By packing with care and considering both the season and your planned activities, you'll be well-equipped to make the most of your time in Tokyo. With the right clothing and essentials, you can focus on experiencing the city's unique blend of tradition and innovation without any worries.

Budgeting Tips for Visiting Tokyo

Budgeting for a trip to Tokyo might seem like a daunting task at first, but with some thoughtful planning and a clear understanding of what to expect, you can enjoy this incredible city without overspending. Tokyo has a reputation for being expensive, and while it does offer luxury options for those who seek them, it's also a city where you can experience a lot on a reasonable budget if you know where to look.

One of your biggest expenses will be accommodation, and Tokyo has options for every budget. If you're looking for something affordable, consider staying in hostels or capsule hotels, which can cost anywhere from 2,000 to 5,000 yen per night. These options are clean, efficient, and uniquely Japanese, offering a comfortable place to rest after a day of exploring. For mid-range travelers, business hotels and boutique accommodations typically range from 8,000 to 15,000 yen per night and often include amenities like Wi-Fi and breakfast. If you're in the mood to splurge, Tokyo offers luxury hotels with stunning views and impeccable service, starting at around 30,000 yen per night. Booking early, especially during peak travel seasons, can help you secure the best rates, and considering accommodations outside central districts can save you money while keeping you connected via Tokyo's excellent public transportation.

Food in Tokyo is another area where you can tailor your spending to suit your budget. If you're dining on a budget, you'll be thrilled by the variety of inexpensive yet delicious options. Convenience stores like 7-Eleven, FamilyMart, and Lawson offer affordable meals, including rice balls, sandwiches, and bento boxes, for as little as 300 to 500 yen. Standing sushi bars and ramen shops are also excellent choices, with meals typically costing between 500 and 1,000 yen. Mid-range dining options, such as izakayas (Japanese pubs) and casual restaurants, usually cost around 1,500 to 3,000 yen per meal, offering great value for money and an authentic culinary experience. If you're celebrating or seeking something special, high-end restaurants can cost anywhere from 10,000 yen to several tens of thousands for a meal. Tokyo's food scene is vast and varied, so you can always find something within your price range while enjoying the city's legendary flavors.

Transportation in Tokyo is surprisingly affordable and incredibly efficient, making it one of the easiest cities to navigate without breaking the bank. The city's extensive train and subway network connects you to virtually every corner of Tokyo. A single journey typically costs 200 to 400 yen, depending on the distance, but purchasing a prepaid Suica or Pasmo card will make your travels more convenient and can help you save a little. For unlimited travel, consider day passes or Tokyo Metro tickets, which range from 600 to 1,500 yen depending on the duration. Taxis, on the other hand, can be quite expensive, so they're best reserved for late nights or special circumstances. Walking is also a great way to save money and discover hidden gems in the city's neighborhoods.

Attractions in Tokyo cater to all budgets, from free experiences to exclusive activities. Many temples, shrines, and parks, such as the iconic Meiji Shrine or the vast grounds of Ueno Park, have no entry fees, allowing you to soak up Tokyo's culture and natural beauty without spending a yen. Museums and galleries often charge modest admission fees, typically between 500 and 1,500 yen, and some offer free entry days or discounts for international visitors. If you're interested in multiple attractions, consider purchasing a pass like the Tokyo Museum Grutto Pass or combination tickets for specific areas. For a splurge-worthy experience, you might visit Tokyo Disneyland or DisneySea, which costs around 8,000 yen per ticket, or ascend the Tokyo Skytree for panoramic city views, with prices starting at 2,100 yen.

To make the most of your budget, there are plenty of money-saving strategies you can use. Look out for lunch specials at restaurants, which often include set meals at lower prices than dinner. Local markets and food stalls are fantastic for sampling delicious, affordable snacks. Take advantage of free or low-cost attractions and events, such as seasonal festivals or public performances. If shopping is on your agenda, head to second-hand stores or outlet malls for great deals. Lastly, planning your trip during the off-season, such as late autumn or winter (excluding New Year's), can help you save on both flights and accommodations.

Tokyo is a city where thoughtful choices go a long way. By balancing your spending between must-see attractions, everyday conveniences, and a few splurges, you can craft an unforgettable experience that fits your budget. With its mix of free activities, affordable food options, and efficient transportation, Tokyo proves that world-class travel doesn't have to come with a sky-high price tag.

Travel Apps and Tools for Tourists in Tokyo

Traveling to Tokyo is an adventure filled with excitement, discovery, and sometimes, challenges. With the right apps and tools, however, you can turn those challenges into opportunities and make your trip smoother, more enjoyable, and less stressful. Tokyo is a modern city where technology is deeply integrated into daily life, and as a traveler, you can benefit immensely by using apps designed to help you navigate, explore, and experience everything the city has to offer.

One of the most essential tools for navigating Tokyo is a reliable map app. Google Maps is incredibly useful for finding your way around the city's complex streets and train networks. It not only provides directions for walking, driving, or cycling but also offers detailed public transportation routes. In a city as busy and interconnected as Tokyo, Google Maps' real-time updates on train schedules, delays, and platform information can save you time and prevent confusion. Another helpful feature is the ability to download maps for offline use, ensuring you're never lost even if you lose internet access.

For transportation, a must-have app is Japan Travel by Navitime. This app is tailored specifically for travelers in Japan and offers comprehensive guidance on navigating the country's public transportation system. In Tokyo, it excels at providing detailed information about train and subway routes, including fare calculations and transfer times. Its ability to display routes in English, along with options to filter by JR Pass eligibility, makes it particularly useful for international visitors. You can also use the app to find nearby stations or plan journeys to specific attractions with step-by-step instructions.

When it comes to dining, Tokyo has no shortage of incredible options, but finding the right place can feel overwhelming. That's where apps like Gurunavi and Tabelog come in. Gurunavi is an excellent resource for discovering restaurants that match your preferences, whether you're looking for sushi, ramen, or vegetarian options. It often includes menus translated into English and provides useful details such as average prices and seating availability. Tabelog, on the other hand, is a popular local app with extensive user reviews, helping you find highly rated eateries that might not appear in tourist guides. Both apps can point you to hidden gems that offer authentic dining experiences.

For exploring Tokyo's vibrant events and attractions, Peatix is an invaluable tool. This app connects you to a wide range of local happenings, from concerts and workshops to cultural festivals and art exhibits. Many events listed on Peatix are off the beaten path, giving you the chance to experience Tokyo beyond its major landmarks. The app is easy to use and often provides options to purchase tickets directly, simplifying your planning.

If you're interested in ride-sharing or taxi services, consider downloading the Uber app or the JapanTaxi app. While Uber is available in Tokyo, it operates primarily as a premium service, so you might find it more economical to use JapanTaxi. This app connects you to Tokyo's extensive fleet of taxis and allows you to book rides, check fares, and even pay through the app. It's especially convenient late at night or in areas where public transportation is less accessible.

Language barriers can sometimes be a concern in Tokyo, but apps like Google Translate can bridge the gap effectively. With features like text translation, photo translation for menus or signs, and even real-time conversation translation, Google Translate is a lifesaver for tourists. By downloading the Japanese language pack for offline use, you'll be prepared for any situation where communication might be tricky.

For those looking to explore Tokyo with confidence and efficiency, HyperDia is another great app for train travel. While similar to Japan Travel by Navitime, HyperDia excels in its detailed breakdown of train schedules and allows you to customize your search to avoid certain lines or minimize travel time. It's particularly useful for planning trips to destinations outside central Tokyo, such as day trips to Nikko or Mount Fuji.

Lastly, apps like Airbnb and Booking.com can help you find accommodations that suit your needs and budget. While these platforms are known globally, they offer features tailored to Tokyo's unique accommodation options, such as capsule hotels, traditional ryokans, and centrally located apartments. Both apps allow you to read reviews, compare prices, and book directly from your phone, making the process seamless.

Having these tools at your fingertips transforms how you experience Tokyo. Instead of worrying about directions, schedules, or language barriers, you can focus on enjoying the city's sights, sounds, and flavors. By combining the convenience of technology with Tokyo's remarkable infrastructure and hospitality, these apps ensure your trip is as effortless as it is memorable. With the right preparation, you'll feel confident navigating Tokyo like a pro, ready to make the most of every moment in this extraordinary city.

CHAPTER 2

GETTING TO AND AROUND TOKYO

Arrival And Departure Information

Arriving in Tokyo is an exciting moment, filled with the anticipation of exploring one of the most dynamic cities in the world. Whether you're stepping off a plane for the first time or returning for another visit, understanding the logistics of arrival and departure can make your experience smoother and less stressful. Tokyo is served by two major international airports, Narita International Airport and Haneda Airport, both of which are well-equipped to handle travelers efficiently and comfortably.

If you're flying into Narita International Airport, located about 60 kilometers (37 miles) east of central Tokyo, you'll arrive at one of Japan's busiest hubs for international travel. Narita has three terminals, each with a clear layout designed to make navigation easy. Terminal 1 is primarily used by major international carriers, Terminal 2 serves a mix of full-service airlines, and Terminal 3 is dedicated to low-cost carriers. Upon arrival, you'll follow signs for immigration, where you'll need your passport and completed landing card. Japan's entry process is efficient, but it's essential to have your documents ready, including a valid visa if required. After clearing immigration, you'll collect your luggage and proceed through customs, where you may need to declare items depending on your belongings.

Haneda Airport, located just 14 kilometers (8.7 miles) from the city center, is Tokyo's other main airport and is known for its convenience and proximity. It has three terminals: Terminals 1 and 2 handle domestic flights, while the International Terminal (Terminal 3) is dedicated to overseas travelers. Haneda is often the preferred choice for those wanting a quick and easy journey into the heart of Tokyo. The immigration and customs procedures at Haneda are similar to those at Narita, with clear signage and helpful staff to guide you through. Having your documents ready and understanding the process ahead of time can help you move through these steps quickly.

Once you've completed the arrival procedures, the next step is getting into Tokyo. From Narita, there are several transportation options to suit different budgets and preferences. The Narita Express (N'EX) train is one of the fastest and most convenient ways to reach central Tokyo, taking about an hour to major stations like Tokyo Station and Shinjuku. It's comfortable and designed for travelers, with luggage storage and reserved seating. If you're looking for a more affordable option, the Keisei Skyliner train is another excellent choice, connecting Narita to Ueno and Nippori stations in around 40 minutes. For budget-conscious travelers, buses are also available and take a bit longer but offer a cheaper way to reach the city.

From Haneda, the transportation options are even more straightforward, thanks to its closer location. The Tokyo Monorail connects Haneda to Hamamatsucho Station in under 15 minutes, where you can transfer to other train lines. Alternatively, Keikyu Railways provides direct train services to major hubs like Shinagawa and Yokohama. Taxis and rideshare services are also readily available at both airports, offering a convenient door-to-door option, though they can be costly compared to public transportation, especially from Narita.

If you're traveling with a lot of luggage or prefer not to navigate public transport, airport limousine buses are a great option. These buses connect both Narita and Haneda to many hotels and major stations in Tokyo. They're comfortable and spacious, with dedicated luggage storage, and can be a more relaxing way to start or end your journey. Car rentals are available at both airports as well, but they're less common for city travel given Tokyo's excellent public transportation and dense traffic.

When it's time to depart Tokyo, the process is just as smooth. Arrive at the airport with enough time to check in, go through security, and complete any departure formalities. Both Narita and Haneda offer excellent facilities to make your wait enjoyable, including duty-free shopping, dining options ranging from quick snacks to full meals, and even cultural experiences like tea ceremonies or art exhibits. Free Wi-Fi is available throughout both airports, so you can stay connected while you wait for your flight.

Understanding your options for arrival and departure ensures you'll feel prepared and confident during your journey to Tokyo. With its world-class airports and efficient transportation systems, the city makes it easy for travelers to begin their adventures on the right note and end their trips smoothly. Whether you're traveling for the first time or returning to rediscover Tokyo's wonders, the experience of arriving and departing is designed to be as seamless as the city itself.

Transportation Options for Getting Around

Getting around Tokyo is an adventure in itself, thanks to the city's efficient and extensive transportation network. Whether you're traveling across bustling districts or exploring quieter neighborhoods, Tokyo offers a range of options to suit every need. With a bit of preparation, navigating the city becomes an enjoyable part of your experience, and you'll soon find yourself moving through Tokyo like a seasoned local.

The subway system is the heart of Tokyo's transportation network, and it's likely to be your main mode of travel. With its vast web of interconnected lines, the subway efficiently connects almost every corner of the city. Operated by two main companies, Tokyo Metro and Toei Subway, the system is clean, safe, and remarkably punctual. To use the subway, you'll first need to purchase a ticket or, more conveniently, a prepaid IC card like Suica or Pasmo. These cards allow you to simply tap in and out at gates without worrying about calculating fares. You can load money onto them at machines found in every station, and they also work on most buses and trains in the region. Navigating the subway might seem overwhelming at first, but apps like Google Maps or Japan Travel by Navitime are invaluable for planning routes and checking schedules in English. Pay attention to the color-coded lines and clear signage, which make it easier to find your way. Traveling during rush hours can be intense, with packed trains and busy platforms, so if you prefer a more relaxed journey, consider avoiding the morning and evening commuter times.

Taxis and rideshare services are another convenient way to get around Tokyo, especially late at night or when carrying heavy luggage. Taxis in Tokyo are known for their reliability and professionalism, with drivers who maintain spotless cars and polite service. You can hail a taxi on the street, find one at designated taxi stands, or book one through apps like JapanTaxi. Keep in mind that taxi fares are higher than public transportation, with base rates starting around 420 yen and additional charges based on distance and time. Rideshare services like Uber are available but operate on a smaller scale and are generally more expensive than taxis. To ensure a smooth experience, have your destination written in Japanese or ready to show on a map, as not all drivers may speak English. Taxis are equipped with automatic doors, so there's no need to open or close them yourself—a small detail that reflects Tokyo's attention to service.

For a broader view of the city and access to areas not served by the subway, Tokyo's public buses are a great option. The bus system might seem less intuitive at first, but with a little patience, it's an efficient way to explore. Buses operate on a flat fare system within central Tokyo, and you can use your Suica or Pasmo card for payment. Stops are announced in Japanese and English, making it easier to know when to get off. Buses are particularly useful for reaching locations like the Tokyo Tower or certain parks and residential areas. If you're near the waterfront, you might also consider taking a ferry along the Sumida River or Tokyo Bay. These ferries offer a relaxing way to travel while enjoying unique views of the city's skyline, bridges, and waterfront attractions.

Walking is one of the simplest and most rewarding ways to explore Tokyo. Many of the city's neighborhoods are best experienced on foot, where you can soak in the atmosphere, discover hidden shops and cafes, and observe everyday life. Districts like Asakusa, Shibuya, and Harajuku are particularly pedestrian-friendly, with plenty of attractions clustered within walking distance. The city is exceptionally clean and safe, making walking a pleasant option for travelers. Comfortable shoes are essential, as you may find yourself walking several kilometers in a day without even realizing it.

While public transportation and walking are ideal for most of Tokyo, there may be times when renting a car is the better choice. Car rentals are useful if you plan to explore areas outside the city, such as Mount Fuji, Nikko, or the Hakone region. Reliable rental companies like Nippon Rent-A-Car and Times Car Rental offer a range of vehicles and can provide English-language support. Rental costs typically start around

6,000 to 10,000 yen per day, and you'll need an International Driving Permit (IDP) to rent and drive in Japan. Driving in Tokyo itself can be challenging due to heavy traffic, narrow streets, and limited parking, so it's generally not recommended unless absolutely necessary. Parking fees can also add up quickly, and many central areas lack affordable parking options. However, for trips to the countryside or scenic drives, renting a car offers the flexibility to explore at your own pace.

Tokyo's transportation options are designed to make travel as seamless and enjoyable as possible, catering to a wide range of preferences and budgets. With its efficient subway, reliable taxis, scenic ferries, and walkable streets, the city invites you to move through it with ease and confidence. Each mode of transport offers a unique perspective on Tokyo, turning even the journey itself into a memorable part of your adventure. By understanding your options and planning ahead, you'll find that getting around Tokyo becomes second nature, leaving you free to focus on experiencing the city's endless wonders.

CHAPTER 3

ACCOMMODATION OPTIONS IN TOKYO

Finding the right place to stay in Tokyo is one of the most important parts of planning your trip. The city offers a wide variety of accommodations to suit every budget, from luxurious hotels with breathtaking views to cozy budget hostels that let you experience Tokyo without breaking the bank. Below, you'll find detailed recommendations for luxury, mid-range, and budget accommodations to help you choose the best fit for your trip.

Luxury Accommodations

For those seeking indulgence and world-class service, Tokyo's luxury hotels deliver on every front. From sweeping views of the skyline to top-notch amenities, these accommodations promise a memorable stay.

The Ritz-Carlton, Tokyo

- **Price Range**: From 100,000 to 150,000 yen per night
- **Amenities**: This five-star hotel offers spacious rooms with panoramic views of Tokyo, a luxurious spa, a 20-meter indoor pool, and Michelin-starred dining options. Complimentary Wi-Fi, concierge service, and an exclusive club lounge enhance your experience.

- **Best Area to Stay**: Located in Roppongi, this hotel is ideal for travelers who want easy access to upscale shopping, fine dining, and vibrant nightlife while enjoying proximity to cultural attractions like the Mori Art Museum.
- **Contact Details**: www.ritzcarlton.com | Phone: +81 3-3423-8000

Aman Tokyo

- **Price Range**: From 130,000 to 200,000 yen per night
- **Amenities**: Known for its minimalist design inspired by traditional Japanese aesthetics, Aman Tokyo provides serene luxury. Highlights include an impressive spa, an infinity pool overlooking the city, and personalized services. The hotel also features a library and an elegant restaurant serving seasonal Japanese cuisine.
- **Best Area to Stay**: Situated in Otemachi, this hotel is perfect for business travelers and those who want easy access to the Imperial Palace and Marunouchi's chic shopping district.
- **Contact Details**: www.aman.com | Email: reservations@aman.com

Park Hyatt Tokyo

- **Price Range**: From 80,000 to 130,000 yen per night
- **Amenities**: Featured in the movie *Lost in Translation*, this iconic hotel boasts spacious rooms with floor-to-ceiling windows, a rooftop pool, a renowned spa, and

impeccable service. Its New York Grill & Bar offers stunning views and a refined dining experience.

- **Best Area to Stay**: Located in Shinjuku, the hotel offers easy access to one of Tokyo's busiest districts, filled with shopping, dining, and entertainment options.
- **Contact Details**: www.hyatt.com | Phone: +81 3-5322-1234

Mid-Range Accommodations

If you're looking for comfort and convenience without the high price tag, Tokyo's mid-range hotels and boutique accommodations are excellent options. They strike the perfect balance between quality and affordability.

Hotel Niwa Tokyo

- **Price Range**: From 15,000 to 25,000 yen per night
- **Amenities**: This charming boutique hotel features stylish, Japanese-inspired interiors, a serene garden courtyard, and a fitness center. Guests enjoy free Wi-Fi, comfortable rooms, and an optional buffet breakfast.
- **Best Area to Stay**: Located in Suidobashi, this hotel is close to Tokyo Dome and offers excellent public transportation connections to major tourist attractions.
- **Contact Details**: www.hotelniwa.jp | Phone: +81 3-3293-0028

Shinjuku Granbell Hotel

- **Price Range**: From 10,000 to 20,000 yen per night
- **Amenities**: This trendy hotel offers modern rooms, a rooftop bar with stunning city views, and an on-site restaurant. Some rooms include kitchenette facilities for added convenience.
- **Best Area to Stay**: Situated in Shinjuku, this hotel places you in the heart of Tokyo's vibrant entertainment district, making it an excellent choice for those who want to explore the nightlife and nearby shopping areas.
- **Contact Details**: www.granbellhotel.jp | Phone: +81 3-5155-2666

Asakusa View Hotel

- **Price Range**: From 12,000 to 18,000 yen per night
- **Amenities**: This hotel offers spacious rooms, some with stunning views of the Tokyo Skytree. Guests can enjoy multiple dining options, including a breakfast buffet and a sky lounge with panoramic vistas.
- **Best Area to Stay**: Located in Asakusa, this hotel is perfect for those who want to experience traditional Tokyo with easy access to Senso-ji Temple and the Sumida River.
- **Contact Details**: www.viewhotels.co.jp | Phone: +81 3-3847-1111

Travelers on a tighter budget will find no shortage of affordable and comfortable options in Tokyo. From hostels to capsule hotels, you can enjoy a pleasant stay without overspending.

Khaosan Tokyo Origami

- **Price Range**: From 3,000 to 5,000 yen per night
- **Amenities**: This friendly hostel offers dormitory and private rooms with free Wi-Fi, shared kitchen facilities, and a communal lounge. The rooftop terrace provides a great spot to relax with views of the Tokyo Skytree.
- **Best Area to Stay**: Situated in Asakusa, this hostel is ideal for budget travelers exploring Tokyo's historic district and its cultural landmarks.
- **Contact Details**: www.khaosan-tokyo.com | Phone: +81 3-3873-7480

Nine Hours Shinjuku-North

- **Price Range**: From 4,000 to 6,000 yen per night
- **Amenities**: This sleek capsule hotel provides futuristic sleeping pods, shared bathrooms, and lockers for secure storage. The minimalist design ensures a clean, comfortable environment.
- **Best Area to Stay**: Located in Shinjuku, this hotel is perfect for travelers who want affordable

accommodations near the city's bustling nightlife and transport hubs.

- **Contact Details**: www.ninehours.co.jp | Phone: +81 3-5291-7337

UNPLAN Shinjuku

- **Price Range**: From 4,500 to 8,000 yen per night
- **Amenities**: This modern hostel offers dormitory and private rooms, free breakfast, a stylish café, and a communal lounge. It's a great place to meet fellow travelers and enjoy a relaxed atmosphere.
- **Best Area to Stay**: Conveniently located in Shinjuku, UNPLAN offers easy access to public transportation, dining, and shopping.
- **Contact Details**: www.unplan.jp | Email: info@unplan.jp

CHAPTER 4

DINING OPTIONS IN TOKYO

Tokyo is a paradise for food lovers, offering an incredible range of culinary experiences that cater to every palate and budget. Whether you're craving traditional Japanese dishes, world-class fine dining, or irresistible street food, Tokyo promises a memorable gastronomic journey. Below, you'll find detailed insights into the city's famous local foods, restaurants across different price ranges, and the vibrant street food scene.

Famous Local Foods

Tokyo is home to some of Japan's most iconic dishes, each reflecting the city's rich culinary heritage and innovative spirit. One must-try is **sushi**, which has its roots in Tokyo (formerly Edo). Edomae sushi, known for its fresh, high-quality fish and vinegared rice, is an experience that every visitor should savor. For an unforgettable meal, visit **Sukiyabashi Jiro** in Ginza, one of the most renowned sushi restaurants in the world, or enjoy more accessible options at **Sushi Dai** in Tsukiji Market.

Another Tokyo staple is **ramen**, a comforting bowl of noodles served in a flavorful broth. Tokyo's ramen scene offers diverse styles, from soy-based shoyu ramen to creamy tonkotsu (pork bone) broth. Try **Ichiran Ramen** in Shinjuku for a personalized dining experience or **Ramen Street** in Tokyo Station, where you can sample bowls from several acclaimed ramen shops.

For a truly local experience, indulge in **tempura**, lightly battered and deep-fried seafood or vegetables. The delicate crunch of tempura is best enjoyed at places like **Tempura Kondo** in Ginza, which combines tradition with modern flair. **Unagi**, or grilled freshwater eel, is another Tokyo delicacy, known for its smoky flavor and savory-sweet glaze. Visit **Nodaiwa** near the Tokyo Tower for a taste of this timeless dish.

Tokyo also excels in **monjayaki**, a savory pancake-like dish filled with a variety of ingredients. It's a Tokyo specialty you can cook yourself on a griddle at spots like **Tsukishima Monja Street**, a haven for monjayaki lovers.

Restaurants by Price Range

Luxury Dining

For an exceptional dining experience, Tokyo's fine dining establishments are unparalleled. **Narisawa**, in Minato, is a two-Michelin-starred restaurant blending Japanese ingredients with French techniques, offering seasonal tasting menus starting at 30,000 yen per person. Another highlight is **Kaiseki Den by Chef Hirohisa Koyama**, where multi-course kaiseki meals feature artfully presented dishes crafted with meticulous attention to detail. Reservations are essential, which can be made through their websites or apps like **TableAll** or **Pocket Concierge**.

If you're seeking the pinnacle of sushi dining, **Sukiyabashi Jiro** in Ginza offers an extraordinary experience for around 40,000 yen per person. Keep in mind that bookings for these luxury venues often require planning well in advance.

Mid-Range Restaurants

For a mix of quality and affordability, mid-range restaurants in Tokyo deliver exceptional value. **Kyubey** in Ginza offers outstanding sushi experiences starting at 10,000 yen, with master chefs preparing each piece before you. For those interested in wagyu beef, **Gyu-An** in Roppongi serves premium teppanyaki-style steak dishes for around 8,000 to 15,000 yen per meal.

Another great choice is **Afuri Ramen**, famous for its yuzu (Japanese citrus) shio ramen, priced at approximately 1,500 yen per bowl. You can find Afuri locations in Harajuku and other parts of Tokyo. Many of these restaurants accept walk-ins, but booking via platforms like **OpenTable** or **Gurunavi** is recommended during peak times.

Budget-Friendly Eateries

Tokyo also caters to those on a budget with countless affordable options. Conveyor-belt sushi chains like **Genki Sushi** in Shibuya offer plates starting at 100 yen each, making it easy to enjoy sushi without spending much. **Matsuya** and

Sukiya serve hearty bowls of gyudon (beef over rice) for under 500 yen, providing a quick and satisfying meal.

For casual ramen, try **Ichiran** or **Ippudo**, where a bowl of noodles costs around 1,000 yen. If you're craving curry, **CoCo Ichibanya** offers customizable curry dishes starting at 800 yen. These budget-friendly eateries are conveniently located throughout Tokyo, and most don't require reservations.

Street Food Recommendations and Food Markets

Tokyo's street food scene is vibrant and full of delicious surprises. Areas like **Ameya-Yokocho Market** in Ueno and **Nakamise Street** in Asakusa are hotspots for sampling local treats. One must-try is **taiyaki**, a fish-shaped pastry filled with sweet red bean paste or custard. Vendors in Asakusa serve some of the best taiyaki, perfect for snacking as you stroll.

Another favorite is **yakitori**, skewered and grilled chicken, which you'll find at stalls and izakayas around **Omoide Yokocho** in Shinjuku. Prices typically range from 100 to 300 yen per skewer, making it an affordable and flavorful option. If you're visiting in cooler months, warm up with **oden**, a comforting hotpot dish available at convenience stores and food stalls.

For a more immersive market experience, head to **Tsukiji Outer Market**, where you can enjoy fresh seafood like uni (sea urchin) or tamagoyaki (sweet rolled omelet) made to order. The market's bustling atmosphere and variety of food make it a must-visit for food enthusiasts. Another excellent destination is **Toyosu Market**, where you can observe the famous tuna auctions and enjoy some of the freshest sushi in Tokyo.

Exploring Tokyo's food markets is not just about eating—it's about immersing yourself in the city's culture. Be sure to bring cash, as many small vendors don't accept credit cards, and arrive early to enjoy the best selections.

Tokyo's dining options are as diverse as its neighborhoods, ensuring there's something for everyone to enjoy. Whether you're savoring a luxurious kaiseki meal, slurping a bowl of ramen, or nibbling on street food at a bustling market, the city's culinary scene is sure to leave a lasting impression. With so many choices, every meal in Tokyo becomes an adventure in flavor and discovery.

CHAPTER 5

TOURIST ATTRACTIONS IN TOKYO

Free Tourist Attractions in Tokyo

Tokyo offers an abundance of free attractions that allow you to explore the city's culture, history, and natural beauty without spending a yen. These sites showcase the diversity and vibrancy of Tokyo, making them perfect for travelers on a budget or anyone seeking unique experiences. Here's a detailed guide to some of the best free attractions in Tokyo.

Meiji Shrine

- **Location**: Located in a lush forest in Shibuya, Meiji Shrine is just a short walk from Harajuku Station on the JR Yamanote Line.
- **Activities**: As one of Tokyo's most iconic Shinto shrines, Meiji Shrine offers a serene escape from the bustling city. You can walk along the tranquil tree-lined pathways leading to the shrine, admire the massive torii gates, and observe traditional ceremonies such as weddings. The inner garden, though requiring a small fee, blooms beautifully in spring and summer, while the public grounds remain free year-round.
- **Best Visiting Times**: Early mornings are the best time to visit for peace and quiet, while weekends often feature

ceremonies that provide insight into Japanese traditions. Visiting during the New Year period (hatsumode) offers a festive and cultural experience, though it can be crowded.

- **Contact Information**: www.meijijingu.or.jp | Phone: +81 3-3379-5511

Senso-ji Temple

- **Location**: Located in Asakusa, Senso-ji Temple is easily accessible via the Asakusa Station on the Tokyo Metro Ginza Line or Toei Asakusa Line.
- **Activities**: Tokyo's oldest Buddhist temple is a must-visit for its historical significance and stunning architecture. You can stroll through the bustling Nakamise Street leading to the temple, filled with souvenir shops and food stalls. The temple grounds are free to explore, and you can admire the impressive five-story pagoda, the Thunder Gate (Kaminarimon), and the main hall.
- **Best Visiting Times**: Mornings and weekdays are ideal for avoiding crowds, while evenings provide a magical atmosphere with the temple beautifully illuminated. Spring offers cherry blossoms in the surrounding area, making it a particularly picturesque time to visit.
- **Contact Information**: www.senso-ji.jp | Phone: +81 3-3842-0181

Ueno Park

- **Location**: Situated near Ueno Station on the JR Yamanote Line, Ueno Park is a sprawling green space in the heart of Tokyo.
- **Activities**: Ueno Park is a cultural and recreational hub. You can wander its beautiful pathways, enjoy seasonal blooms like cherry blossoms in spring, and visit the open-air spaces around historical landmarks like the Kiyomizu Kannon Temple and the Saigo Takamori Statue. While some museums in the park charge admission, the park itself and many of its outdoor attractions are free. Street performances and food stalls often add to the lively atmosphere.
- **Best Visiting Times**: Spring, during cherry blossom season, is the park's most famous time, but fall also offers stunning foliage. Weekdays and early mornings are quieter, especially during peak seasons.
- **Contact Information**: www.ueno-bunka.jp | Phone: +81 3-3828-5644

Tokyo Metropolitan Government Building Observation Decks

- **Location**: Located in Shinjuku, a 10-minute walk from Shinjuku Station on the JR and Tokyo Metro lines.
- **Activities**: The Tokyo Metropolitan Government Building offers free access to its observation decks, located on the 45th floor. From here, you can enjoy panoramic views of the city, including landmarks like

Tokyo Tower, Tokyo Skytree, and even Mount Fuji on clear days. The North Deck is open later, making it perfect for night views of the city's glittering skyline.

- **Best Visiting Times**: Arrive early in the morning or late in the evening for fewer crowds and the best visibility. Winter mornings are ideal for spotting Mount Fuji, thanks to clearer skies.
- **Contact Information**: www.metro.tokyo.jp | Phone: +81 3-5321-1111

Tsukiji Outer Market

- **Location**: Near Tsukiji Station on the Tokyo Metro Hibiya Line, the Outer Market surrounds the former inner fish market area.
- **Activities**: While the inner wholesale market has relocated to Toyosu, the Outer Market remains a bustling hub of activity. You can explore its narrow lanes filled with food stalls, fresh seafood, and cooking equipment shops. Browsing the market is free, though you might be tempted to sample some street food like tamagoyaki (sweet omelet) or grilled seafood.
- **Best Visiting Times**: Visit early in the morning for the freshest produce and to experience the vibrant market atmosphere. Many shops close by early afternoon, so plan your visit accordingly.
- **Contact Information**: www.tsukiji.or.jp | Phone: +81 3-3541-9444

Yoyogi Park

- **Location**: Adjacent to Harajuku Station on the JR Yamanote Line, Yoyogi Park is a vast public space in central Tokyo.
- **Activities**: This park is perfect for a leisurely stroll, a picnic, or people-watching. On weekends, you'll often encounter musicians, performers, and cosplayers showcasing their talents. The park is especially popular during cherry blossom season and for its vibrant ginkgo trees in autumn.
- **Best Visiting Times**: Visit on weekends for lively events and performances or early mornings for a peaceful walk. Spring and autumn offer the best scenery, but the park is enjoyable year-round.
- **Contact Information**: www.yoyogipark.jp | Phone: +81 3-3469-6081

Imperial Palace East Gardens

- **Location**: A short walk from Otemachi or Tokyo Station on various subway and JR lines.
- **Activities**: The East Gardens of the Imperial Palace are free to the public and offer a glimpse into Japan's history. You can explore the remains of Edo Castle, scenic ponds, and beautifully landscaped gardens. Informational plaques provide insights into the site's significance.
- **Best Visiting Times**: Visit in the late morning or early afternoon when the gardens are fully open. Spring and autumn bring seasonal highlights like cherry blossoms

and colorful foliage. The gardens are closed on Mondays and Fridays.

- **Contact Information**: www.kunaicho.go.jp | Phone: +81 3-3213-1111

Odaiba's Waterfront

- **Location**: Accessible via the Yurikamome Line to Odaiba-Kaihinkoen Station.
- **Activities**: Odaiba offers a stunning waterfront view of Tokyo Bay, complete with attractions like the Rainbow Bridge and a replica Statue of Liberty. Enjoy a relaxing walk along the beach area or explore the futuristic architecture of the surrounding buildings. The area is also a great spot for sunset views and cityscape photography.
- **Best Visiting Times**: Evenings are ideal for enjoying the illuminated bridge and skyline, while weekends bring a lively atmosphere with local events.
- **Contact Information**: www.tokyo-odaiba.net | Phone: +81 3-5531-0818

These free attractions highlight Tokyo's rich culture, history, and natural beauty, ensuring you can enjoy the city without overspending. Whether you're admiring sweeping views, exploring ancient temples, or relaxing in scenic parks, Tokyo's diverse offerings promise unforgettable experiences for every traveler.

Paid Tourist Attractions in Tokyo

Tokyo is a treasure trove of captivating landmarks and world-class museums, offering countless opportunities to dive into the city's rich culture, history, and modernity. While some attractions come at a cost, the experiences they offer are well worth the price, promising unforgettable memories. Below is a detailed guide to some of Tokyo's must-visit paid attractions, divided into iconic landmarks and museum recommendations.

Iconic Landmarks

Tokyo Skytree

- **Description**: Rising 634 meters above the city, Tokyo Skytree is the tallest structure in Japan and a modern symbol of Tokyo. It offers breathtaking panoramic views from its observation decks and houses a shopping complex, an aquarium, and restaurants.
- **Entry Prices**: Tickets to the Tembo Deck (350 meters) start at 2,100 yen for adults, with a combined ticket for the Tembo Galleria (450 meters) available for 3,100 yen. Discounts are offered for children, and tickets can be purchased online for convenience.
- **Activities**: You can enjoy 360-degree views of Tokyo, including landmarks like Mount Fuji on clear days. At night, the city lights create a dazzling spectacle. The lower levels feature shopping and dining, including a Michelin-starred restaurant.

- **Best Visiting Times**: Early mornings and weekdays are the best times to avoid crowds. Visiting during sunset offers a magical transition from day to night views.
- **Contact Information**: www.tokyo-skytree.jp | Phone: +81 3-5302-3470

Tokyo Tower

- **Description**: Modeled after the Eiffel Tower, Tokyo Tower stands at 333 meters and is a beloved symbol of the city. Its vibrant orange-and-white structure is iconic, and it offers stunning views of the Tokyo skyline.
- **Entry Prices**: Tickets for the Main Deck (150 meters) cost 1,200 yen, while combined access to the Top Deck (250 meters) costs 3,000 yen. Discounts are available for children and groups. Tickets can be booked online to save time.
- **Activities**: Explore the observation decks for sweeping views of the city, visit the FootTown area for shopping and dining, or enjoy light shows and seasonal events.
- **Best Visiting Times**: Visit in the evening to see the city illuminated. Weekdays are less crowded than weekends.
- **Contact Information**: www.tokyotower.co.jp | Phone: +81 3-3433-5111

Odaiba and TeamLab Borderless

- **Description**: Odaiba, an artificial island in Tokyo Bay, is home to futuristic attractions, including the interactive digital art museum, TeamLab Borderless. This museum features immersive, ever-changing light and art installations.
- **Entry Prices**: Tickets for TeamLab Borderless cost 3,200 yen for adults and 1,000 yen for children. Advance booking online is required, as slots fill up quickly.
- **Activities**: Explore mesmerizing art installations, walk through a world of colors and lights, and take Instagram-worthy photos. The surrounding Odaiba area offers shopping malls, waterfront views, and attractions like the Rainbow Bridge.
- **Best Visiting Times**: Book morning slots to avoid crowds and fully enjoy the immersive exhibits.
- **Contact Information**: www.teamlab.art | Email: info@teamlab.art

Shibuya Sky

- **Description**: Located atop the Shibuya Scramble Square building, Shibuya Sky is an open-air observation deck offering incredible views of Shibuya Crossing and the wider Tokyo skyline.
- **Entry Prices**: Admission costs 2,000 yen for adults, with discounts for children. Tickets are cheaper when booked online in advance.

- **Activities**: Watch the famous Shibuya Crossing from above, enjoy rooftop seating with skyline views, and visit the indoor Sky Gallery for interactive exhibits.
- **Best Visiting Times**: Sunset offers spectacular views as the city transitions to night. Book in advance to secure your preferred time slot.
- **Contact Information**: www.shibuya-scramble-square.com

Museum Recommendations

Edo-Tokyo Museum

- **Description**: This museum offers an in-depth look at Tokyo's transformation from the Edo period to the modern era through immersive exhibits, life-sized replicas, and artifacts.
- **Entry Prices**: Tickets cost 600 yen for adults, with discounts for students and seniors. Children under elementary school age enter free.
- **Special Exhibits**: The museum frequently hosts special exhibitions, focusing on Edo-era culture, architecture, and samurai history.
- **Best Visiting Times**: Mornings and weekdays are quieter, allowing you to explore at your own pace.
- **Contact Information**: www.edo-tokyo-museum.or.jp | Phone: +81 3-3626-9974

Ghibli Museum

- **Description**: A dream for Studio Ghibli fans, this whimsical museum in Mitaka showcases the art and imagination behind films like *My Neighbor Totoro* and *Spirited Away*.
- **Entry Prices**: Tickets cost 1,000 yen for adults, 700 yen for students, and 400 yen for children. Tickets must be purchased in advance online or through designated outlets.
- **Special Exhibits**: Rotating exhibits delve into the creative process behind Studio Ghibli's beloved films.
- **Best Visiting Times**: Early morning slots offer a quieter experience. The museum is especially magical during autumn and winter.
- **Contact Information**: www.ghibli-museum.jp | Phone: +81 570-055-777

Mori Art Museum

- **Description**: Located in Roppongi Hills, this contemporary art museum features cutting-edge exhibitions and a rooftop observation deck with incredible city views.
- **Entry Prices**: General admission costs 1,800 yen, with discounts for students and children. Combo tickets for the museum and observation deck are also available.
- **Special Exhibits**: The museum regularly hosts exhibitions by renowned international artists.

- **Best Visiting Times**: Evenings provide a quieter atmosphere and stunning views from the rooftop.
- **Contact Information**: www.mori.art.museum | Phone: +81 3-6406-6652

National Museum of Emerging Science and Innovation (Miraikan)

- **Description**: This hands-on museum in Odaiba explores cutting-edge science and technology, featuring interactive exhibits and demonstrations.
- **Entry Prices**: Tickets are 630 yen for adults and 210 yen for students. Children under six enter for free.
- **Special Exhibits**: Topics include robotics, space exploration, and renewable energy. Don't miss the humanoid robots and dome theater.
- **Best Visiting Times**: Weekdays and early afternoons are less crowded.
- **Contact Information**: www.miraikan.jst.go.jp | Phone: +81 3-3570-9151

From towering landmarks to world-class museums, Tokyo's paid attractions offer something for everyone. Whether you're marveling at city views from above or delving into history and art, these experiences will add depth and excitement to your journey through this vibrant metropolis.

Guided Tours in Tokyo

Exploring Tokyo on a guided tour is one of the best ways to immerse yourself in the city's vibrant culture, history, and modern energy. Whether you prefer walking through historic neighborhoods, cycling along the city's streets, or savoring local cuisine, there's a tour for every interest. Guided tours in Tokyo offer the expertise of knowledgeable guides who can help you uncover hidden gems and gain deeper insights into this fascinating metropolis. Here's an extensive guide to the types of tours available, complete with practical details to help you choose the perfect experience.

Walking Tours

Walking tours are an intimate and immersive way to explore Tokyo's neighborhoods and landmarks, allowing you to connect with the city at street level. These tours often focus on specific themes, such as history, culture, or architecture.

Description: On a walking tour, you'll traverse areas like Asakusa, where Senso-ji Temple and Nakamise Street come alive with history, or Harajuku, where quirky fashion and street art take center stage. Guided commentary brings context to the sights, offering stories and cultural insights that you might miss on your own.

Examples of Tour Operators:

- **Tokyo Free Walking Tour**: A volunteer-based service offering pay-as-you-wish tours of iconic spots like the Imperial Palace and Asakusa.
- **Tokyo Localized**: Offers curated tours of historic districts and hidden local spots.

Price Range: Free to 5,000 yen per person, depending on the tour and whether tips are encouraged.

Amenities Provided: Guided commentary, maps, and recommendations for further exploration.

Contact Information:

- Tokyo Free Walking Tour: www.tfwt.jp | Email: contact@tfwt.jp
- Tokyo Localized: www.tokyolocalized.com

Additional Tips: Wear comfortable shoes and bring water, as these tours often involve walking several kilometers. Morning tours are ideal for cooler temperatures and fewer crowds.

Bus Tours

Bus tours are perfect if you want to cover a lot of ground in a short amount of time. They provide a comfortable way to see Tokyo's major landmarks with the added benefit of a knowledgeable guide or audio commentary.

Description: These tours typically take you to must-see spots like Tokyo Tower, Meiji Shrine, and Odaiba, offering guided insights along the way. Some tours include stops at attractions like the Imperial Palace or Tokyo Skytree, allowing you to explore on foot before continuing your journey.

Examples of Tour Operators:

- **Hato Bus**: A well-established company offering a variety of themed tours, including city highlights and seasonal cherry blossom routes.
- **Japan Panoramic Tours**: Offers hop-on, hop-off bus options for flexible sightseeing.

Price Range: 5,000 to 10,000 yen per person, with discounts for children and groups.

Amenities Provided: Air-conditioned buses, multilingual guides or audio commentary, and optional meal packages.

Contact Information:

- Hato Bus: www.hatobus.com | Phone: +81 3-3761-1100
- Japan Panoramic Tours: www.jptours.co.jp

Additional Tips: Afternoon tours are great for avoiding morning rush hour traffic. Bring a camera for photo stops and check whether meals or admission tickets are included in the tour package.

Bike Tours

Bike tours offer a unique way to explore Tokyo's neighborhoods, parks, and waterfront areas. They combine sightseeing with light exercise, making them ideal for active travelers.

Description: These tours often include routes through scenic areas like the Imperial Palace Gardens, Sumida River, or Odaiba. Guides ensure safety while sharing fascinating stories about the landmarks you pass.

Examples of Tour Operators:

- **Tokyo Miracle Cycling Tour**: Known for personalized small-group tours around the city's quieter streets and hidden gems.
- **Freewheeling Japan**: Offers guided tours with an emphasis on cultural immersion.

Price Range: 4,000 to 8,000 yen per person, including bike rentals.

Amenities Provided: Bicycle rental, helmets, safety instructions, and guided commentary.

Contact Information:

- Tokyo Miracle Cycling Tour: www.tokyomiraclecycling.com
- Freewheeling Japan: www.freewheeling.jp

Additional Tips: Opt for tours in the morning or late afternoon to avoid peak heat during summer. Wear comfortable clothing and bring sunscreen.

Specialty Tours

Specialty tours cater to specific interests, such as food, history, or cultural experiences. These tours often provide deeper insights into Tokyo's unique offerings.

Food Tours

Description: Dive into Tokyo's culinary world by exploring local eateries, food markets, and specialty shops. You might sample sushi, ramen, or wagashi (traditional sweets) while learning about Japanese food culture.

Examples of Tour Operators:

- **Arigato Japan**: Offers themed food tours in neighborhoods like Tsukiji, Asakusa, and Shibuya.
- **Magical Trip**: Focuses on street food and nightlife tours.
  Price Range: 8,000 to 12,000 yen per person, including food tastings.
  Contact Information:
- Arigato Japan: www.arigatojapan.co.jp | Email: info@arigatojapan.co.jp

Historical Tours

Description: Uncover Tokyo's past with visits to Edo-era sites, samurai districts, or WWII landmarks. Guides bring history to life with captivating stories.

Examples of Tour Operators:

- **Samurai Walk**: Focuses on samurai history in areas like Nihonbashi.
- **Historical Tokyo Tours**: Covers Edo-era landmarks and Meiji Restoration sites. **Price Range**: 5,000 to 8,000 yen per person.

Adventure Tours

Description: Adventure tours offer unique experiences, such as sumo wrestler meet-and-greets, sake brewery visits, or even ninja training.

Examples of Tour Operators:

- **InsideJapan Tours**: Offers behind-the-scenes experiences with local experts.
- **Ninja Tokyo**: Provides immersive ninja workshops for all ages. **Price Range**: 10,000 to 20,000 yen, depending on the activity.

Additional Tips for Specialty Tours: Book well in advance, especially for high-demand experiences like food tours or seasonal activities. Wear comfortable clothing and bring a small bag for any purchases or souvenirs.

Whether you prefer exploring on foot, pedaling through scenic streets, or diving into Tokyo's rich culture and cuisine, guided tours offer something for everyone. With knowledgeable guides and well-organized itineraries, you'll gain a deeper appreciation of the city while enjoying stress-free sightseeing. Whatever your interest, a guided tour in Tokyo is a rewarding way to experience this incredible city.

Day Trip Recommendations And Excursions

Tokyo is a city that never ceases to amaze, but some of the most memorable experiences lie just beyond its borders. Day trips from Tokyo offer a chance to explore Japan's stunning countryside, historic towns, and serene coastal regions, all within a few hours of travel. Whether you're seeking cultural landmarks, natural beauty, or seasonal events, these excursions provide a perfect complement to your time in the capital. Here's a detailed guide to nearby destinations, transportation options, and seasonal tips to help you plan the ultimate day trips from Tokyo.

Nearby Destinations

Venturing outside Tokyo reveals a diverse array of destinations, each with its own unique charm. From ancient temples to picturesque beaches, you'll find something to suit every interest.

One of the most popular day trips is to **Nikko**, a historic town Located in the mountains. Known for its UNESCO World Heritage sites, including the ornate Toshogu Shrine, Nikko immerses you in Japan's rich history and spiritual traditions. The Kegon Falls and Lake Chuzenji add to its natural allure, particularly during the autumn months when the foliage transforms into a vibrant tapestry of red and gold. To reach Nikko, take the Tobu Railway from Asakusa Station, a journey of about two hours costing approximately 2,700 yen round trip. Spring and fall are the best times to visit, with cherry blossoms and autumn leaves creating stunning backdrops.

For those seeking a coastal escape, **Kamakura** is a delightful destination. Often called the Kyoto of Eastern Japan, Kamakura is home to the iconic Great Buddha (Daibutsu) and serene Zen temples such as Hase-dera. Stroll along Komachi Street to sample traditional sweets and shop for souvenirs. The beaches of Kamakura also provide a relaxing setting, particularly in summer. You can reach Kamakura in just under an hour from Tokyo Station via the JR Yokosuka Line, with tickets costing about 920 yen each way. Visit in early summer for hydrangea blooms or in winter for clear views of Mount Fuji.

Another must-visit location is **Hakone**, famous for its hot springs, art museums, and views of Mount Fuji. You can ride the Hakone Ropeway, cruise across Lake Ashi, and unwind in an onsen. The Hakone Freepass, available for around 5,000 yen, offers unlimited travel on local transportation and discounts on attractions. From Shinjuku Station, take the Odakyu Romancecar to Hakone-Yumoto, a journey of about 90 minutes costing 2,300 yen one way. Spring and autumn are ideal seasons, with cherry blossoms and colorful foliage enhancing the landscape.

For wine lovers, **Yamanashi Prefecture**, just two hours from Tokyo, is a hidden gem. The Katsunuma region is dotted with vineyards offering wine tastings and tours. Many wineries, such as Chateau Mercian, provide breathtaking views of the surrounding mountains. Take the Limited Express Azusa train from Shinjuku to Katsunuma-budokyo Station, with tickets costing around 3,500 yen one way. Fall is the best season to visit, coinciding with the grape harvest and wine festivals.

For a truly unique experience, consider **Yokohama**, a port city blending modern attractions with a rich maritime history. Stroll through the historic Red Brick Warehouse, explore the Cup Noodles Museum, or take in panoramic views from the Landmark Tower's observation deck. Yokohama is just 30 minutes from Tokyo by train, with round-trip tickets costing less than 1,000 yen. This destination is ideal year-round, but summer offers lively waterfront events and festivals.

Transportation Options for Da Trips

Tokyo's transportation network makes it incredibly easy to explore nearby destinations, with reliable trains, buses, and rental cars providing flexible options for every traveler.

The most convenient and popular mode of transport for day trips is the **train**. Japan's rail system is fast, punctual, and well-connected, with the JR lines and private railways covering most destinations near Tokyo. Consider purchasing a regional rail pass, such as the JR Tokyo Wide Pass (10,000 yen for three days of unlimited travel), which offers great value for multi-day excursions. Apps like Navitime or Google Maps can help you plan routes and schedules with ease.

For those heading to less accessible locations, **buses** are an excellent alternative. Highway buses offer direct routes to destinations like Mount Fuji, with fares starting around 2,000 yen each way. Companies like Willer Express and JR Bus provide comfortable seats, Wi-Fi, and online booking options. The Shinjuku Expressway Bus Terminal is a major hub for departures.

If you prefer the freedom of your own itinerary, **car rentals** are widely available in Tokyo. Rental companies like Nippon Rent-A-Car and Times Car Rental offer competitive rates starting at 6,000 yen per day, plus fuel and tolls. An International Driving Permit (IDP) is required, and driving conditions in Japan are well-regulated. Renting a car is especially useful for exploring rural areas like Yamanashi or Hakone at your own pace.

Navigating the transportation systems is straightforward, but it's wise to book tickets in advance during peak seasons or weekends. For trains, reserving seats on limited express services ensures a stress-free journey. Additionally, packing light and bringing a portable Wi-Fi device can enhance your travel experience.

The time of year plays a significant role in shaping your day trip experience. Certain destinations are best visited during specific seasons to fully appreciate their beauty and charm.

Spring is one of the most magical times to explore areas like Nikko and Kamakura, where cherry blossoms create breathtaking scenery. Popular spots like the Shinjuku Gyoen or Ueno Park can be crowded, so early morning departures are recommended to beat the rush.

Summer brings vibrant festivals and coastal escapes. Kamakura's beaches and Yokohama's waterfront come alive with lively events, making them perfect for a day of fun in the sun. However, summer heat can be intense, so pack sunscreen, a hat, and plenty of water.

Autumn is ideal for exploring mountainous regions like Hakone and Nikko, where the fall foliage transforms the landscape into a palette of warm colors. This season also coincides with harvest festivals in Yamanashi's wine country, offering a unique cultural and culinary experience.

Winter offers clear skies and crisp air, making destinations like Mount Fuji and Yokohama particularly picturesque. Hot springs in Hakone are especially inviting during the colder months, providing a relaxing way to warm up after a day of sightseeing.

Day trips from Tokyo offer an incredible range of experiences, from historic temples and coastal adventures to wine tastings and hot springs. With efficient transportation options and stunning seasonal highlights, these excursions provide the perfect escape from the city while adding depth and variety to your Tokyo adventure. By planning ahead and considering the best times to visit, you'll ensure a memorable journey beyond the bustling capital.

CHAPTER 6

ADVENTURE ACTIVITIES IN TOKYO

Tokyo is not just a bustling metropolis of neon lights and towering skyscrapers; it also offers a diverse range of outdoor activities that connect you to nature, adventure, and relaxation. From serene gardens to adrenaline-pumping adventures, Tokyo's outdoor offerings cater to every type of traveler. Whether you're an avid hiker, a water sports enthusiast, or simply looking for a peaceful escape, the city has something to offer. Here's an inspiring guide to the best outdoor activities you can enjoy in and around Tokyo.

Hiking and Nature Walks

If you're craving a break from the city's fast pace, Tokyo is home to stunning trails and nature walks that provide an escape into serene, green landscapes. These spots range from gentle strolls through lush parks to challenging hikes with rewarding views.

Mount Takao

Mount Takao is one of Tokyo's most popular hiking destinations, located just an hour from the city center. Its trails cater to all skill levels, from paved paths for beginners to more rugged routes for seasoned hikers. The most popular trail, Trail 1, takes about 90 minutes to ascend and leads to breathtaking views of Tokyo and, on clear days, Mount Fuji. Along the way, you'll encounter the Yakuoin Temple, which adds a cultural touch to the hike.

- **Amenities**: Picnic areas, restrooms, and restaurants are available near the summit and at the base.
- **Entry**: Free, though the cable car and chair lift cost around 500–1,000 yen for a one-way ride.
- **Contact Information**: www.takaotozan.co.jp | Phone: +81 42-661-4151

Meiji Shrine Inner Garden

For a more leisurely nature walk, the Meiji Shrine's Inner Garden offers a peaceful retreat in the heart of Tokyo. Stroll along shaded paths lined with towering trees and discover tranquil ponds, historic monuments, and seasonal flower displays. The Iris Garden is particularly stunning in June.

- **Trail Duration**: Approximately 30–45 minutes.
- **Entry Fee**: 500 yen per person.
- **Contact Information**: www.meijijingu.or.jp

Showa Kinen Park

Located in Tachikawa, this expansive park features sprawling lawns, colorful flower gardens, and cycling paths. It's a fantastic spot for families, offering playgrounds, picnic areas, and a boating lake. Seasonal highlights include cherry blossoms in spring and vibrant autumn foliage.

- **Entry Fee**: 450 yen per adult.
- **Contact Information**: www.showakinen-koen.jp

Water-Based Activities

Tokyo's waterways and coastal areas provide unique opportunities for water-based adventures, from tranquil boating excursions to thrilling sports on the bay.

Kayaking in Odaiba

Paddle through Tokyo's futuristic skyline with a kayaking adventure in Odaiba. The calm waters around the Rainbow Bridge and Odaiba Seaside Park make this activity suitable for beginners and experienced kayakers alike.

- **Rental and Tour Costs**: Approximately 5,000–8,000 yen for a two-hour guided tour.
- **Best Time to Visit**: Summer and early autumn for pleasant weather and warm water.
- **Contact Information**: Odaiba Kayak Tour: www.tokyokayaktour.com

Boating on the Sumida River

Explore Tokyo's historic districts from a new perspective with a boat tour along the Sumida River. Many tours depart from Asakusa and offer scenic views of landmarks like Tokyo Skytree and the Rainbow Bridge. Options range from traditional yakatabune boats, which include meals, to modern river cruises.

- **Cost**: 1,500–6,000 yen depending on the tour package.
- **Contact Information**: Tokyo Cruise: www.suijobus.co.jp

Beach Day in Enoshima

Just an hour from Tokyo, Enoshima offers sandy beaches perfect for relaxing or trying paddleboarding. The island itself is a treasure trove of small shrines, scenic viewpoints, and seafood restaurants.

- **Rental Costs for Water Sports**: Paddleboard rental starts at 3,000 yen for two hours.
- **Contact Information**: www.enoshima-kayak.com

Adventure Sports

For adrenaline seekers, Tokyo and its surroundings offer thrilling activities that will make your heart race while immersing you in Japan's natural beauty.

Rock Climbing at Bouldering Tokyo

Try your hand at indoor bouldering in the city or head to natural climbing sites just outside Tokyo, such as Mount Mitake. These experiences cater to all skill levels and provide a mix of physical challenge and fun.

- **Cost**: Indoor climbing gyms start at 2,000 yen for a day pass, with gear rental available. Outdoor climbing tours can range from 10,000–15,000 yen.
- **Contact Information**: www.boulderingtokyo.com

Zip-lining in Tama Hills

Tama Hills offers a high-flying adventure with zip-lining and treetop obstacle courses, perfect for families and groups. This activity combines thrills with stunning views of Tokyo's surrounding forests.

- **Cost**: 5,000 yen for a half-day experience.
- **Contact Information**: Forest Adventure: www.forestadventure.jp

Relaxed Outdoor Experiences

Not all outdoor activities have to be high-energy. Tokyo also excels in providing serene, leisurely options that let you soak in the city's beauty at your own pace.

Shinjuku Gyoen National Garden

One of Tokyo's most beautiful parks, Shinjuku Gyoen is perfect for picnics, photography, or a relaxing walk. Its vast grounds feature French, English, and traditional Japanese gardens, creating a tranquil oasis in the heart of the city.

- **Entry Fee**: 500 yen per adult.

- **Best Time to Visit**: Spring for cherry blossoms or autumn for colorful foliage.
- **Contact Information**: www.env.go.jp

Tokyo Outdoor Markets

Spend a leisurely afternoon browsing Tokyo's outdoor markets, such as the Oedo Antique Market in Yurakucho or the United Nations University Farmers' Market in Aoyama. You'll find unique souvenirs, fresh produce, and plenty of local treats to sample.

- **Entry Fee**: Free to explore, with items available for purchase.
- **Best Time to Visit**: Weekend mornings for the liveliest atmosphere.

Scenic Drives to Mount Fuji

For a relaxed adventure with stunning views, consider renting a car and driving to the Mount Fuji Five Lakes area. The journey takes about two hours from central Tokyo and offers scenic stops along the way, including parks and viewpoints.

- **Cost**: Car rentals start at 6,000 yen per day, plus fuel and tolls.
- **Contact Information**: Nippon Rent-A-Car: www.nipponrentacar.co.jp

Tips for Enjoying Tokyo's Outdoors

- **Clothing**: Dress in layers and wear comfortable, weather-appropriate clothing.
- **Essentials**: Bring water, sunscreen, and a hat for sun protection.
- **Gear**: Consider renting equipment like bikes or kayaks rather than bringing your own.
- **Timing**: Early mornings and weekdays are often quieter, offering a more peaceful experience.

Tokyo's outdoor activities provide a perfect blend of adventure, nature, and relaxation. With so many options to explore, you'll find it easy to step outside the urban bustle and experience the natural beauty and unique charm of the city

Activities For Solo Tourists

Traveling solo in Tokyo is an enriching experience, offering endless opportunities to explore the city at your own pace. Tokyo is incredibly welcoming to solo travelers, with safe spaces, efficient transportation, and activities that cater to both introverts seeking solitude and extroverts eager to connect with others. Below, you'll find a guide to attractions perfect for solo adventurers, followed by thoughtfully crafted itineraries for 3-day, 7-day, and 14-day stays.

Attractions for Solo Travelers

Tokyo has countless attractions designed for solo exploration, from cultural landmarks to unique experiences that let you enjoy the city's charm independently.

Senso-ji Temple

- **Details**: Located in Asakusa, Senso-ji is Tokyo's oldest Buddhist temple and a must-visit for its stunning architecture and vibrant atmosphere. Solo travelers can comfortably wander Nakamise Street, lined with souvenir shops and food stalls, before entering the temple grounds.
- **Pricing**: Free entry. Food and souvenirs on Nakamise Street range from 200 to 1,000 yen.
- **Best Times to Visit**: Early mornings for a serene experience or evenings to see the temple illuminated.
- **Contact Information**: www.senso-ji.jp | Phone: +81 3-3842-0181

Tokyo Skytree

- **Details**: Enjoy breathtaking panoramic views of the city from the Skytree's observation decks. Solo travelers can book a guided audio tour to learn about Tokyo's landmarks. The surrounding Solamachi shopping complex offers dining and entertainment options.
- **Pricing**: Observation deck tickets start at 2,100 yen.
- **Best Times to Visit**: Sunset for stunning cityscapes or weekday mornings to avoid crowds.

- **Contact Information**: www.tokyo-skytree.jp | Phone: +81 3-5302-3470

Ghibli Museum

- **Details**: This whimsical museum dedicated to Studio Ghibli's animated films is perfect for solo travelers who love art and storytelling. Enjoy exhibits and screenings of short films exclusive to the museum.
- **Pricing**: Tickets cost 1,000 yen and must be purchased in advance.
- **Best Times to Visit**: Weekday mornings or early afternoons for a quieter experience.
- **Contact Information**: www.ghibli-museum.jp | Phone: +81 570-055-777

Ueno Park

- **Details**: A spacious park perfect for solo walks, Ueno Park is home to museums, a zoo, and seasonal cherry blossoms. It's a great spot to relax, take photos, or people-watch.
- **Pricing**: Free to enter. Museum admission fees range from 500 to 1,000 yen.
- **Best Times to Visit**: Spring for cherry blossoms or early mornings for quiet strolls.
- **Contact Information**: www.ueno-bunka.jp

Cooking Classes and Food Tours

- **Details**: Join a cooking class to learn how to make sushi, ramen, or wagashi (traditional sweets). Food tours in neighborhoods like Tsukiji or Asakusa are also ideal for solo travelers, offering small-group settings to connect with others while enjoying local cuisine.
- **Pricing**: Classes start at 5,000 yen, and food tours range from 8,000 to 12,000 yen.
- **Best Times to Visit**: Lunchtime or evenings for food tours.
- **Contact Information**:
  Arigato Japan: www.arigatojapan.co.jp

Suggested Itineraries for Solo Travelers

Whether you're staying for a few days or weeks, these itineraries provide a balanced mix of sightseeing, cultural experiences, and downtime to help you make the most of your solo adventure.

3-Day Itinerary: Highlights of Tokyo

Day 1

- Morning: Visit Senso-ji Temple and explore Nakamise Street.
- Afternoon: Head to Ueno Park for a leisurely walk and visit the Tokyo National Museum.

- Evening: Enjoy a traditional meal at an izakaya (Japanese pub) in Asakusa.

Day 2

- Morning: Experience the bustling Tsukiji Outer Market and join a food tour.
- Afternoon: Take in city views from Tokyo Skytree's observation deck and explore Solamachi.
- Evening: Wander through the neon-lit streets of Shinjuku and visit Omoide Yokocho for casual dining.

Day 3

- Morning: Relax in Meiji Shrine and Yoyogi Park.
- Afternoon: Shop in Harajuku and Omotesando.
- Evening: End your trip with a view from Shibuya Sky.

7-Day Itinerary: Exploring Tokyo and Beyond

Day 1-3

- Follow the 3-day itinerary.

Day 4

- Morning: Visit the Edo-Tokyo Museum to learn about the city's history.
- Afternoon: Stroll through Ginza's upscale shops and art galleries.

- Evening: Watch a kabuki performance at Kabukiza Theatre.

Day 5

- Full Day: Take a day trip to Kamakura to see the Great Buddha and Zen temples. Enjoy the coastal scenery and explore Komachi Street.

Day 6

- Morning: Explore Akihabara's anime and gaming culture.
- Afternoon: Discover Asakusa's hidden spots or join a guided bike tour.
- Evening: Relax in an onsen (hot spring) at Odaiba.

Day 7

- Full Day: Visit TeamLab Borderless in Odaiba and enjoy a cruise along Tokyo Bay.

14-Day Itinerary: Immersive Tokyo Experience

Day 1-7

- Follow the 7-day itinerary.

Day 8

- Full Day: Take a day trip to Nikko to visit Toshogu Shrine, Kegon Falls, and Lake Chuzenji.

Day 9

- Morning: Explore Shimokitazawa's vintage shops and trendy cafes.
- Afternoon: Visit the Mori Art Museum in Roppongi.
- Evening: Dine at a Michelin-starred restaurant in Shinjuku.

Day 10

- Morning: Visit the Tokyo Imperial Palace East Gardens.
- Afternoon: Enjoy a sushi-making class.
- Evening: Stroll through the illuminated Rikugien Garden.

Day 11-12

- Overnight Trip: Travel to Hakone to relax in hot springs and see Mount Fuji. Visit the Hakone Open-Air Museum and enjoy the Hakone Ropeway.

Day 13

- Morning: Return to Tokyo and visit the Ameya-Yokocho Market in Ueno.
- Afternoon: Take a traditional tea ceremony workshop.
- Evening: Explore nightlife in Ebisu or Roppongi.

Day 14

- Morning: Relax at Shinjuku Gyoen National Garden.

- Afternoon: Shop for souvenirs in Ikebukuro's Sunshine City.
- Evening: Enjoy a farewell dinner in Tokyo Tower's restaurant with views of the city.

Final Tips for Solo Travelers

- **Transportation**: Use a prepaid Suica or Pasmo card for seamless travel on trains and buses.
- **Lodging**: Opt for capsule hotels or hostels with communal areas to meet fellow travelers.
- **Safety**: Tokyo is incredibly safe, but always keep an eye on your belongings.
- **Connections**: Join group tours or classes to interact with locals and other tourists.

Activities For Couple Tourists.

Tokyo is an enchanting city that effortlessly blends the charm of ancient traditions with the allure of modern romance. For couples, the city offers countless ways to create lasting memories, from serene gardens and intimate dining spots to thrilling adventures and breathtaking views. Whether you're celebrating an anniversary, honeymoon, or simply sharing a special trip, Tokyo provides the perfect backdrop for love to flourish. Below, you'll find a detailed guide to romantic attractions and thoughtfully crafted itineraries for couples, no matter the length of your stay.

Tokyo is brimming with romantic spots and activities designed to bring couples closer together. These attractions are perfect for quiet moments, shared adventures, and unforgettable experiences.

Tokyo Skytree

- **Details**: As Japan's tallest structure, Tokyo Skytree offers couples an unforgettable panoramic view of the city, especially during sunset or at night when Tokyo sparkles with lights. The Skytree's Tembo Galleria is an ideal spot for romantic photos. Afterward, enjoy a cozy dinner at one of the restaurants in the Solamachi complex.
- **Pricing**: Observation deck tickets start at 2,100 yen per person. Restaurant costs vary, with casual and fine dining options available.
- **Best Times to Visit**: Sunset or evening for magical views of the illuminated city.
- **Contact Information**: www.tokyo-skytree.jp | Phone: +81 3-5302-3470

Rikugien Garden

- **Details**: Known as one of Tokyo's most beautiful traditional gardens, Rikugien is perfect for a romantic stroll. The landscaped paths, charming tea houses, and seasonal highlights like cherry blossoms in spring or glowing autumn foliage set a serene and intimate atmosphere.

- **Pricing**: Entry is 300 yen per person.
- **Best Times to Visit**: Spring for cherry blossoms and autumn for vibrant leaves. Evening illuminations during these seasons add to the romance.
- **Contact Information**: www.tokyo-park.or.jp

Tokyo Bay Cruise

- **Details**: A cruise along Tokyo Bay offers couples a dreamy evening on the water. Many cruises include gourmet dining, drinks, and live entertainment. The Rainbow Bridge and city skyline provide a stunning backdrop, especially during sunset or under a starry sky.
- **Pricing**: Dinner cruises start around 10,000 yen per person.
- **Best Times to Visit**: Evening cruises are the most romantic, with dazzling city views.
- **Contact Information**: Symphony Cruise: www.symphony-cruise.co.jp | Phone: +81 3-3798-8101

Odaiba and TeamLab Borderless

- **Details**: Explore the magical, immersive digital art installations of TeamLab Borderless with your partner. Wander hand-in-hand through rooms of ever-changing lights, colors, and patterns. The nearby Odaiba waterfront is perfect for a romantic walk afterward.
- **Pricing**: Tickets are 3,200 yen per person and must be booked online in advance.

- **Best Times to Visit**: Evening slots enhance the magical atmosphere.
- **Contact Information**: www.teamlab.art | Email: info@teamlab.art

Hot Springs (Onsen) in Hakone

- **Details**: For ultimate relaxation, take a day trip or overnight excursion to Hakone. Many onsen resorts offer private baths where couples can soak together while enjoying views of Mount Fuji or the surrounding forests.
- **Pricing**: Day-use onsen starts at 2,000 yen per person, with private onsen rentals from 5,000 yen.
- **Best Times to Visit**: Winter for cozy warmth in the hot springs.
- **Contact Information**: Hakone Yuryo: www.hakoneyuryo.jp

Suggested Itineraries for Couples

Whether you're in Tokyo for a few days or two weeks, these itineraries are crafted to balance sightseeing, romance, and relaxation, ensuring every moment is memorable.

3-Day Itinerary: A Romantic Tokyo Getaway

Day 1

- Morning: Begin with a peaceful stroll through Meiji Shrine and Yoyogi Park.

- Afternoon: Visit Harajuku's quirky shops and enjoy a romantic lunch at an Omotesando café.
- Evening: Head to Shibuya Sky for a sunset view and explore the bustling streets of Shibuya.

Day 2

- Morning: Take a guided tour of Senso-ji Temple and explore Nakamise Street.
- Afternoon: Enjoy an elegant lunch cruise on Tokyo Bay.
- Evening: Relax with a couple's spa treatment or visit an onsen in Odaiba.

Day 3

- Morning: Visit Rikugien Garden for a serene walk.
- Afternoon: Explore Akihabara or Ginza for shopping and sightseeing.
- Evening: Dine at a Michelin-starred restaurant in Ginza or Shinjuku.

7-Day Itinerary A Week of Romance and Discovery

Day 1-3

- Follow the 3-day itinerary.

Day 4

- Morning: Take a day trip to Kamakura to see the Great Buddha and explore Zen temples.

- Afternoon: Stroll along Komachi Street, sampling local delicacies.
- Evening: Return to Tokyo and enjoy dinner at a rooftop restaurant in Roppongi.

Day 5

- Morning: Discover the whimsical world of the Ghibli Museum in Mitaka.
- Afternoon: Visit Inokashira Park for a romantic boat ride on the lake.
- Evening: Experience the magic of TeamLab Borderless.

Day 6

- Full Day: Take a day trip to Hakone. Enjoy the ropeway, visit Lake Ashi, and relax in a private onsen.

Day 7

- Morning: Return to Tokyo and explore Tsukiji Outer Market.
- Afternoon: Spend a leisurely afternoon at Shinjuku Gyoen.
- Evening: Celebrate your last night with a dinner cruise on Tokyo Bay.

14-Day Itinerary: A Dreamy Tokyo Experience

Day 1-7

- Follow the 7-day itinerary.

Day 8

- Full Day: Take a day trip to Nikko to explore the ornate Toshogu Shrine and enjoy the stunning natural beauty of Kegon Falls.

Day 9

- Morning: Explore Shimokitazawa's trendy shops and cozy cafés.
- Afternoon: Visit the Edo-Tokyo Museum for a historical journey.
- Evening: Dine at a themed restaurant like Alice in Fantasy Book in Ginza.

Day 10-11

- Overnight Trip: Head to the Mount Fuji Five Lakes area. Visit the Chureito Pagoda for iconic views and stay at a luxury ryokan with a private onsen.

Day 12

- Morning: Return to Tokyo and enjoy a sushi-making class together.
- Afternoon: Wander through the illuminated streets of Ginza.
- Evening: Watch a kabuki performance at Kabukiza Theatre.

Day 13

- Full Day: Explore the historical streets of Kawagoe, known as "Little Edo."
- Evening: Enjoy a quiet dinner in Tokyo's Ebisu neighborhood.

Day 14

- Morning: Relax with a leisurely breakfast at your hotel.
- Afternoon: Shop for souvenirs in Ikebukuro or Omotesando.
- Evening: Conclude your trip with a romantic dinner at Tokyo Tower's restaurant.

Final Tips for Couples

- **Accommodations**: Choose boutique hotels or ryokan with private onsen for a romantic atmosphere.
- **Transportation**: Use the JR Pass or regional rail passes for day trips and easy navigation.
- **Dining**: Book in advance for popular restaurants, especially for sunset or skyline views.

Family-Friendly Activities

Tokyo is a vibrant city that welcomes families with open arms, offering an incredible variety of activities to delight children and parents alike. From interactive museums and world-class theme parks to serene gardens and kid-friendly dining spots, Tokyo provides countless opportunities to create lasting family memories. Below, you'll find an extensive guide to family-friendly attractions and carefully designed itineraries to make your visit seamless and enjoyable.

Attractions for Families with Kids

Tokyo is packed with family-friendly attractions designed to entertain and educate children while keeping parents comfortable. These destinations feature interactive exhibits, play areas, and facilities tailored to the needs of families.

Tokyo Disneyland and DisneySea

- **Details**: These iconic theme parks are the ultimate family destinations. Tokyo Disneyland features classic Disney attractions and characters, while DisneySea offers unique adventures with a nautical twist. Both parks include kid-friendly rides, character meet-and-greets, and plenty of dining options.
- **Pricing**: One-day tickets start at 8,200 yen for adults and 4,900 yen for children (ages 4–11). Family packages and multi-day tickets are available.
- **Amenities**: Stroller rentals, nursing rooms, baby food options, and themed play areas.
- **Best Times to Visit**: Weekdays during off-peak seasons (January–March or September–November) to avoid crowds. Arrive early for shorter wait times.
- **Contact Information**: www.tokyodisneyresort.jp | Phone: +81 45-330-5211

- **Details**: Japan's oldest zoo is home to over 3,000 animals, including pandas, tigers, and elephants. The spacious grounds include a monorail ride and picnic areas, making it a hit with kids.
- **Pricing**: Admission is 600 yen for adults, 200 yen for children (ages 12–18), and free for children under 12.
- **Amenities**: Stroller rentals, restrooms with changing tables, and food stalls.
- **Best Times to Visit**: Mornings or weekdays for a quieter experience. Spring offers beautiful cherry blossoms in the surrounding park.
- **Contact Information**: www.tokyo-zoo.net | Phone: +81 3-3828-5171

National Museum of Nature and Science (Ueno)

- **Details**: This hands-on museum features kid-friendly exhibits on dinosaurs, space, and Japanese ecosystems. Children will love the life-sized dinosaur skeletons and interactive displays.
- **Pricing**: Admission is 630 yen for adults and free for children under 18.
- **Amenities**: Family rest areas, stroller access, and a café with kid-friendly meals.
- **Best Times to Visit**: Mornings or late afternoons during weekdays.
- **Contact Information**: www.kahaku.go.jp | Phone: +81 3-5777-8600

Legoland Discovery Center

- **Details**: Located in Odaiba, this indoor attraction features Lego-themed rides, workshops, and play zones perfect for younger kids. Adults can join the fun or relax in the café.
- **Pricing**: Tickets start at 2,500 yen for both adults and children (advance purchase recommended). Children under 2 enter for free.
- **Amenities**: Nursing rooms, rest areas, and a café.
- **Best Times to Visit**: Weekday mornings to avoid crowds.
- **Contact   Information**: www.legolanddiscoverycenter.jp/tokyo

Ghibli Museum

- **Details**: Families can immerse themselves in the magical worlds of Studio Ghibli at this whimsical museum. Kids will love climbing on Totoro statues and exploring interactive exhibits inspired by films like *My Neighbor Totoro*.
- **Pricing**: Admission is 1,000 yen for adults and 400 yen for children (ages 4–12). Tickets must be purchased in advance.
- **Amenities**: Stroller parking, a children's play area, and a themed café.
- **Best Times to Visit**: Early mornings or weekdays for a quieter experience.
- **Contact Information**: www.ghibli-museum.jp | Phone: +81 570-055-777

Suggested Itineraries for Families

Traveling with kids requires thoughtful planning, and these tailored itineraries ensure a perfect balance of fun and relaxation. Designed with family-friendly attractions, dining, and transportation tips, they'll help you make the most of your time in Tokyo.

3-Day Itinerary: Family Highlights

Day 1

- Morning: Start your trip at Ueno Zoo. Let the kids enjoy animal encounters and take the monorail for fun views.
- Afternoon: Have a family picnic in Ueno Park, followed by a visit to the National Museum of Nature and Science.
- Evening: Dine at a casual family-friendly restaurant in Akihabara, such as CoCo Ichibanya for customizable curry.

Day 2

- Morning: Spend the day at Tokyo Disneyland. Focus on rides and attractions suitable for young children, such as Pooh's Hunny Hunt and It's a Small World.

- Evening: Watch the nighttime parade and fireworks before heading back to your hotel.

Day 3

- Morning: Visit the Legoland Discovery Center in Odaiba.
- Afternoon: Stroll along Odaiba's waterfront, stopping for ice cream at Aqua City.
- Evening: Enjoy a relaxing family dinner at a themed restaurant like the Robot Restaurant in Shinjuku.

7-Day Itinerary: A Week of Family Fun

Day 1-3: Follow the 3-day itinerary.

Day 4

- Morning: Explore the Ghibli Museum in Mitaka.
- Afternoon: Take a boat ride on the nearby Inokashira Park lake.
- Evening: Relax with a simple dinner near your accommodation.

Day 5

- Full Day: Take a day trip to Hakone. Ride the Hakone Ropeway, visit the Open-Air Museum, and enjoy a family-friendly onsen.

Day 6

- Morning: Visit the Edo-Tokyo Museum to learn about Japan's history in an engaging way.
- Afternoon: Explore Asakusa's Nakamise Street for snacks and souvenirs.
- Evening: Enjoy a casual dinner at a conveyor-belt sushi restaurant.

Day 7

- Morning: Relax in Shinjuku Gyoen National Garden.
- Afternoon: Spend the afternoon at Sunshine City in Ikebukuro, where kids can enjoy the aquarium or planetarium.

14-Day Itinerary: A Comprehensive Family Adventure

Day 1-7: Follow the 7-day itinerary.

Day 8

- Morning: Take a day trip to Kamakura to visit the Great Buddha and enjoy the beach.
- Evening: Return to Tokyo for dinner at a family-friendly izakaya.

Day 9

- Full Day: Spend the day at Tokyo DisneySea for nautical-themed attractions.

Day 10-11

- Overnight Trip: Travel to Nikko for a mix of history and nature. Visit Toshogu Shrine, enjoy the waterfalls, and stay at a ryokan with family amenities.

Day 12

- Morning: Return to Tokyo and visit the Tokyo Skytree.
- Afternoon: Explore the Solamachi complex for shopping and kid-friendly dining.

Day 13

- Morning: Take a cooking class to learn how to make Japanese dishes together.
- Afternoon: Visit Odaiba's TeamLab Borderless for an immersive art experience.

Day 14

- Morning: Relax at Meiji Shrine and Yoyogi Park.
- Afternoon: Shop for souvenirs in Harajuku and Omotesando.
- Evening: Celebrate your last night with a memorable meal at a family-friendly restaurant like Ninja Akasaka.

Final Tips for Family Travel

- **Transportation**: Use a prepaid Suica or Pasmo card for convenient travel. Children receive discounted fares.
- **Meals**: Many restaurants offer kids' menus or customizable options.
- **Packing**: Bring snacks, water, and small toys to keep kids entertained during downtime.

Tokyo is a city full of family-friendly adventures that make traveling with kids a joy. With careful planning and these tailored suggestions, you can look forward to a trip filled with laughter, learning, and cherished memories.

GROUP ACTIVITIES

Traveling to Tokyo with a group can be an exhilarating experience. The city offers a variety of group-friendly activities, from guided tours and cultural workshops to spacious dining venues and interactive entertainment. Whether you're planning a short trip or a longer stay, Tokyo caters to groups with ease, offering memorable experiences that foster connection, collaboration, and fun. Below is a comprehensive guide to group-friendly tours, venues, and itineraries, ensuring a seamless and enjoyable visit for your group.

Recommendations for Group-Friendly Tours and Venues

Tokyo has an abundance of tours and venues designed to accommodate groups, offering private options, group discounts, and amenities that enhance the experience for everyone.

Tokyo Tower Group Tour

- **Details**: Tokyo Tower offers private group tours that include access to the observation decks and a guided introduction to its history. Groups can enjoy a shared experience of breathtaking views of the city, making it a perfect icebreaker or celebratory activity.
- **Pricing**: Observation deck tickets start at 1,200 yen per person. Group discounts are available for parties of 20 or more.
- **Amenities**: Dedicated group check-in, private tours, and dining options in the tower's restaurants.
- **Best Times to Visit**: Weekday mornings for smaller crowds and clearer views.
- **Contact Information**: www.tokyotower.co.jp | Phone: +81 3-3433-5111

Samurai and Ninja Experience at Edo Wonderland

- **Details**: Edo Wonderland in Nikko offers immersive experiences where your group can dress as samurai or ninja and participate in team-building activities like archery, swordsmanship, and stealth techniques.

- **Pricing**: Admission starts at 4,800 yen per person, with discounts for groups of 15 or more. Costume rentals and guided workshops are additional.
- **Amenities**: Large group spaces, professional instructors, and photo packages.
- **Best Times to Visit**: Spring and autumn for pleasant weather and outdoor activities.
- **Contact Information**: www.edowonderland.net | Phone: +81 288-77-1777

TeamLab Borderless Private Group Tour

- **Details**: Experience the world-famous digital art museum, TeamLab Borderless, in Odaiba. Groups can book private time slots for exclusive access to the immersive exhibits, ensuring everyone gets a chance to explore and take photos.
- **Pricing**: Standard tickets are 3,200 yen per person, with private group packages available upon request.
- **Amenities**: Exclusive group entry, customizable schedules, and guides for larger groups.
- **Best Times to Visit**: Evenings for a more magical atmosphere and fewer crowds.
- **Contact Information**: www.teamlab.art | Email: info@teamlab.art

Sumo Stable Tour and Lunch

- **Details**: Visit a sumo training stable to watch wrestlers practice and learn about this fascinating aspect of Japanese culture. Groups can enjoy a chanko nabe (hot pot) meal together afterward, mirroring the diet of sumo wrestlers.
- **Pricing**: Tours with lunch start at 10,000 yen per person. Discounts available for groups of 10 or more.
- **Amenities**: Private group seating for meals and exclusive Q&A sessions with wrestlers.
- **Best Times to Visit**: Morning practices during sumo tournament seasons (January, May, September).
- **Contact Information**: www.sumo.or.jp

Ginza Sushi Workshop

- **Details**: Book a private sushi-making workshop in Ginza, where your group can learn from master chefs and create your own sushi. This hands-on activity encourages collaboration and is perfect for groups looking to bond over food.
- **Pricing**: Starts at 7,000 yen per person, with discounts for larger groups.
- **Amenities**: Private kitchen space, all materials provided, and group photos.
- **Best Times to Visit**: Late mornings or afternoons for lunch sessions.
- **Contact Information**: www.sushiworkshop.jp

Suggested Itineraries for Groups

Planning for a group can be complex, but these thoughtfully crafted itineraries ensure a balance of activities, relaxation, and opportunities for connection. Each itinerary is tailored to maximize your time in Tokyo while accommodating group dynamics.

3-Day Itinerary: Highlights for Groups

Day 1

- Morning: Begin with a private group tour of Tokyo Tower. Take in the views and enjoy a team breakfast at one of the nearby cafés.
- Afternoon: Head to Asakusa to visit Senso-ji Temple and shop along Nakamise Street.
- Evening: Enjoy a group dinner cruise on Tokyo Bay with Symphony Cruise, offering stunning nighttime views of the city.

Day 2

- Morning: Explore TeamLab Borderless with a private group booking.
- Afternoon: Have lunch at DiverCity Tokyo Plaza, followed by group-friendly shopping.
- Evening: Dine at a themed restaurant like Ninja Akasaka for a fun and interactive meal.

Day 3

- Morning: Visit Ueno Zoo or the National Museum of Nature and Science, both ideal for group exploration.
- Afternoon: Relax at Shinjuku Gyoen National Garden with a group picnic.
- Evening: Conclude with a sushi-making workshop in Ginza.

7-Day Itinerary: A Week of Exploration

Day 1-3: Follow the 3-day itinerary.

Day 4

- Full Day: Take a day trip to Hakone for onsen (hot springs) relaxation, a cruise on Lake Ashi, and team-building activities at the Hakone Open-Air Museum.

Day 5

- Morning: Explore the Edo-Tokyo Museum for a historical perspective on the city.
- Afternoon: Attend a private tea ceremony workshop, offering an immersive cultural experience.
- Evening: Enjoy a group dinner in Roppongi with a view of the skyline.

Day 6

- Morning: Visit Meiji Shrine and Yoyogi Park for a serene start to the day.

- Afternoon: Spend the afternoon in Harajuku, shopping and exploring quirky attractions.
- Evening: Relax with an izakaya dinner in Shinjuku, featuring shared small plates.

Day 7

- Full Day: Take a day trip to Kamakura to visit the Great Buddha and explore Zen temples.

14-Day Itinerary: A Comprehensive Group Adventure

Day 1-7: Follow the 7-day itinerary.

Day 8

- Morning: Travel to Nikko for a full-day tour of Toshogu Shrine, Lake Chuzenji, and Kegon Falls.
- Evening: Return to Tokyo and enjoy a group dinner at a local soba restaurant.

Day 9

- Morning: Visit Akihabara for group gaming and anime shopping.
- Afternoon: Take part in a calligraphy or ikebana (flower arranging) workshop.
- Evening: Explore the nightlife in Ebisu or Shibuya.

Day 10-11

- Overnight Trip: Head to Mount Fuji and the Five Lakes area for hiking, sightseeing, and relaxing at a ryokan with group accommodations.

Day 12

- Morning: Return to Tokyo and visit Tsukiji Outer Market for a guided food tour.
- Afternoon: Wander through Odaiba and enjoy attractions like the Ferris wheel.

Day 13

- Morning: Relax at Rikugien Garden.
- Afternoon: Enjoy a private group wine-tasting experience at a Yamanashi vineyard.

Day 14

- Morning: Shop for souvenirs in Ginza or Omotesando.
- Afternoon: Wrap up with a group lunch at a rooftop café.
- Evening: Celebrate your last night with a dinner cruise on Tokyo Bay.

Final Tips for Group Travel

- **Transportation**: Use chartered buses or purchase group rail passes for convenient travel.

- **Meals**: Book restaurants with private dining rooms or large seating areas.
- **Flexibility**: Plan downtime between activities to allow for group recovery and casual bonding.

Tokyo's dynamic mix of attractions ensures that groups can enjoy a variety of activities that cater to all interests and preferences. With these suggestions, your group will leave Tokyo with cherished memories and stronger connections.

CULTURAL ETIQUETTE IN TOKYO

Understanding the cultural etiquette in Tokyo will help you navigate the city with respect and ease. Tokyo, like much of Japan, has a set of social customs that are deeply ingrained in daily life, and paying attention to these customs will make your visit more pleasant and show respect to the local culture. Whether you're dining at a restaurant, riding a train, or visiting a temple, being aware of the local norms will enhance your experience and help you avoid any unintentional faux pas. This section covers two important aspects of Tokyo's cultural etiquette: **Tipping Norms** and **Expected Behavior in Public Spaces**.

Tipping Norms in Tokyo

In Tokyo, tipping is not a common practice and can even be considered rude in some situations. The Japanese culture values humility and respect, and employees in the service industry are typically paid a fair wage that does not rely on tips. Therefore, tipping is generally not expected or necessary. However, there are certain exceptions, and knowing how to navigate tipping practices can help you avoid awkwardness and show appreciation in the right way.

1. Tipping in Restaurants

- **General Rule**: Tipping in restaurants is **not customary** in Tokyo. If you leave a tip, it may be seen as a misunderstanding or even an insult because it can suggest that the staff need extra money to do their job. Service charges are already included in the price of food and drinks, so there is no need to add more.
- **Exception**: In high-end or luxury establishments, such as top-tier hotels or private dining experiences, you may see a service charge added to your bill. In such cases, no further tip is required.

2. Tipping in Taxis

- **General Rule**: There is **no need to tip** taxi drivers in Tokyo. Taxi fares are metered, and the price you see on the meter is the total amount you owe. While taxi drivers in Japan are known for their impeccable service, tipping is not part of the culture.
- **Customary Behavior**: If you would like to show extra appreciation, you can express your thanks with a polite "Arigato gozaimasu" (thank you very much) when exiting the taxi. If you do want to give something extra,

it is best to place it in an envelope to avoid any discomfort.

3. Tipping Hotel Staff

- **General Rule**: In Tokyo, tipping hotel staff—whether bellhops, concierge, or housekeeping—is not expected. Hotel staff take pride in providing excellent service without the expectation of additional payment.
- **Exception**: In some very high-end hotels or ryokan (traditional inns), a small gift or token of appreciation, such as a bottle of wine or fruit, may be left. However, this is not a requirement and is purely voluntary.

4. Tipping Tour Guides

- **General Rule**: Tipping tour guides in Tokyo is not standard practice. Tour guides usually have a fixed salary and do not expect additional tips. However, if you feel that the guide went above and beyond to ensure your experience was exceptional, a small gift or card of thanks may be appreciated.
- **Note**: It's important to give gifts discreetly in Japan, so consider handing the item over in private rather than in front of the group to avoid causing any embarrassment.

5. How to Tip (If You Really Want To)
If you do find a situation where tipping is appropriate, here are a few tips on how to do it respectfully:

- **Discreet**: If you choose to leave a tip, it is customary to place the money in an envelope or neatly fold it and present it with both hands. This shows respect and humility.

- **Avoid tipping directly**: If you are unsure about the tipping norms, it's better to refrain from tipping. Instead, offer a simple, heartfelt "thank you" or a small gift as a gesture of appreciation.

In summary, while tipping is generally not expected in Tokyo, small gestures of gratitude, like thanking service staff, are appreciated.

Expected Behavior in Public Spaces

Tokyo is a city that places a high value on respect, courtesy, and orderliness. When visiting public spaces, it's essential to follow these norms to avoid any social discomfort and to blend in with the local culture. Here's what you need to know about expected behavior when out and about in Tokyo.

1. Respectful Conduct in Public Spaces

- **Noise Levels**: Tokyo is a bustling metropolis, but the Japanese take pride in maintaining quiet and calm in public spaces. When riding public transportation, in elevators, or in public areas such as museums, it is important to speak in a low voice and avoid making loud phone calls. Keep conversations quiet, especially in quieter spaces like libraries, temples, or gardens.

- **Queuing**: Japanese culture places great emphasis on orderly behavior, and queuing is no exception. You will find clear lines at train stations, bus stops, and elevators. It's important to stand in line and wait your turn without pushing or cutting in line. When waiting for trains, always stand on the designated platform markers and allow passengers to exit before boarding.
- **Interacting with Locals**: Japanese people tend to be reserved and polite, especially when meeting strangers. Be respectful of personal space and avoid being overly familiar. A polite bow or a simple "sumimasen" (excuse me) goes a long way in initiating conversation.

2. Dress Codes

- **General Dress Norms**: In Tokyo, people tend to dress neatly and conservatively, especially in public spaces. While there is no strict dress code for most places, you'll find that Japanese people tend to err on the side of modesty and elegance.
- **Religious and Cultural Sites**: When visiting religious sites like temples and shrines, it's important to dress respectfully. Avoid wearing shorts or revealing clothing; modest, comfortable attire is preferred. If you are visiting a shrine, remove your hat and bow your head slightly as a sign of respect.
- **Seasonal Dress**: Tokyo has four distinct seasons, and how you dress will depend on the time of year. Summer can be hot and humid, so light, breathable fabrics are best. In winter, temperatures can drop, and warm, layered clothing is advisable.

3. Photography Etiquette

- **Public Spaces**: Photography is generally acceptable in public spaces like parks, streets, and shopping districts, but always be mindful of your surroundings. In some crowded areas, such as temples, shrines, or museums, photography may be prohibited. Always look for signs or ask before snapping photos in these areas.
- **Private Spaces**: In private areas, such as in restaurants or on private property, it is courteous to ask permission before taking photos. Avoid taking pictures of people without their consent, especially in more personal settings, like local homes or shops.
- **Respectful Framing**: While photographing landscapes or street scenes, avoid capturing people without their knowledge, especially in intimate settings like temples or quiet areas. When in doubt, always ask for permission.

4. Customs and Traditions

- **Greetings**: In Japan, the most common greeting is a bow. While shaking hands has become more common, especially in business settings, bowing remains a deep-rooted custom. A simple, polite "Konnichiwa" (hello) or "Arigato" (thank you) is appropriate for most occasions.
- **Gestures to Avoid**: Some gestures that are common in Western cultures may be seen as rude in Japan. For example, avoid pointing at people or objects. Instead, gesture with your whole hand or fingers together to be

more polite. Additionally, raising your voice or using overly dramatic body language can be seen as disrespectful.

Final Thoughts

Being mindful of Tokyo's cultural etiquette will not only enhance your travel experience but also help you forge meaningful connections with locals. By respecting the quiet public spaces, following proper tipping customs, and dressing appropriately for the occasion, you will immerse yourself in the Japanese way of life and be seen as a respectful visitor. These small gestures of thoughtfulness and respect will make your time in Tokyo even more rewarding.

SAFETY AND EMERGENCY INFORMATION

Tokyo is one of the safest cities in the world, but like any large, bustling metropolis, it's important to be aware of your surroundings and prepared for unexpected situations. While crime rates are low and public services are efficient, knowing how to stay safe in crowded areas and understanding what to do in case of an emergency will ensure your trip remains smooth and stress-free. This section will guide you through practical safety tips and provide essential emergency contact information, giving you the confidence to explore Tokyo with peace of mind.

Safety Tips for Crowded Areas

Tokyo is known for its vibrant energy and high population density, especially in popular districts like Shibuya, Shinjuku, Asakusa, and Ginza. While these areas are exciting and full of life, they can also be overwhelming at times. Here's how to stay safe while navigating the crowds.

1. Protecting Your Personal Belongings Tokyo is remarkably safe in terms of crime, but like any major city, petty theft (such as pickpocketing) can occur, especially in crowded or tourist-heavy areas. Here are some simple steps to protect your belongings:

- **Use a money belt or neck pouch**: Keep your valuables, such as cash, passport, and credit cards, close to your body. A money belt worn under your clothes or a neck pouch can help you carry important items discreetly and securely.
- **Use zippered bags**: When carrying a bag, make sure it has zippers and keep it tightly closed, especially in busy markets, subway stations, or on crowded streets. Avoid leaving bags unattended.
- **Avoid carrying large amounts of cash**: Most shops and restaurants in Tokyo accept credit or debit cards.

Carry just enough cash for daily expenses and leave the rest in a safe place, such as a hotel safe.

- **Be cautious in crowded public transport**: On crowded trains, be mindful of your personal space. Keep your phone, wallet, and other valuables securely in your pockets or bag.

2. Navigating Crowds

Tokyo is known for its rush-hour crowds, especially during weekdays when office workers flood the train stations. Here's how to manage the crowds and stay safe:

- **Avoid peak hours**: If possible, try to avoid the busiest times of the day—typically between 7:30 AM and 9:00 AM, and 5:30 PM and 7:00 PM. Travel earlier in the morning or later in the evening to experience a more relaxed commute.
- **Stay alert and keep your bearings**: In crowded areas like Shibuya Crossing or Ueno Park, it can be easy to get lost in the flow of people. Keep an eye on signs and landmarks so you don't lose track of where you are. If you're unsure of your direction, ask for help—Tokyo residents are very helpful and often speak some level of English.
- **Maintain personal space**: While Tokyoites are used to large crowds, it's polite to avoid pushing or jostling others. If you need to move through a crowd, make sure to do so gently and respectfully.
- **Plan escape routes in emergencies**: In any crowded area, it's a good idea to know where the nearest exits or open spaces are, just in case you need to leave quickly.

3.   **Staying**   **Connected**

Staying in touch with someone you trust and keeping your phone charged can be lifesaving in unfamiliar situations. Here's how to ensure you stay connected:

- **Share your itinerary**: Before heading out, share your daily itinerary and plans with a friend or family member. Let them know where you'll be going and when you plan to return, especially if you're traveling alone.
- **Keep your phone charged**: Make sure to keep your phone charged throughout the day. Carry a portable charger (power bank) with you so that you always have access to maps, emergency contacts, and communication in case of any issues.
- **Use local SIM cards or Wi-Fi**: If you're traveling from abroad, consider getting a local SIM card or a portable Wi-Fi device. This ensures you can always access your phone's map, emergency services, or translation apps while you're out and about.

4. General Safety Tips for Busy Areas

- **Stay in well-lit areas at night**: Tokyo is generally very safe, but it's always good practice to stick to well-lit areas when walking at night. Avoid alleyways and quiet streets, especially in less frequented parts of the city.
- **Be cautious with strangers**: While most people in Tokyo are friendly and helpful, it's wise to remain cautious when approached by strangers asking for

money, personal information, or assistance. Always trust your instincts.

- **Keep your hotel details handy**: Always have your hotel address written in Japanese. In case you need assistance, it will be easier for taxi drivers, emergency services, or locals to understand where you are staying.

Emergency Contact Information

In the unlikely event that you need help, it's crucial to know the key emergency contacts in Tokyo. Here's the essential information you should have on hand to handle emergencies with ease.

1.   Emergency   Numbers   in   Tokyo
If you find yourself in an emergency situation, here are the key numbers you'll need:

- **Police**: Dial **110** for police assistance in an emergency. This is the number for reporting crimes, accidents, or situations where you need police intervention.
- **Medical Assistance / Ambulance**: Dial **119** for an ambulance or fire emergency. If you or someone else needs medical help, this is the number to call for immediate medical response.
- **Fire**: Dial **119** for fire emergencies. This number also connects you to ambulances, so it's good to remember in case of any emergency.

2. Embassies and Consulates

If you lose your passport or need assistance as a foreigner, contacting your embassy or consulate is the first step. Here's contact information for major embassies in Tokyo:

- **U.S. Embassy:**
  Address: 1-10-5 Akasaka, Minato City, Tokyo
  Phone: +81 3-3224-5000
  Website: https://jp.usembassy.gov
- **British Embassy:**
  Address: 1-1-2, Akasaka, Minato City, Tokyo
  Phone: +81 3-5211-1100
  Website:
  https://www.gov.uk/world/organisations/british-embassy-tokyo
- **Australian Embassy:**
  Address: 2-1-14, Mita, Minato City, Tokyo
  Phone: +81 3-5232-4111
  Website: https://japan.embassy.gov.au
- **Canadian Embassy:**
  Address: 7-3-38 Akasaka, Minato-ku, Tokyo
  Phone: +81 3-5412-6200
  Website:
  https://www.canadainternational.gc.ca/japan-japon/index.aspx

3. Traveler Assistance Services

For general traveler assistance, including lost items, translations, or safety concerns, consider using these services:

- **Japan National Tourist Organization (JNTO)**: Website: https://www.japan.travel/en/ They offer help with emergency information, lost property, and general travel queries.
- **Tokyo Metropolitan Police Safety Hotline**: Phone: **#9110** (for non-emergencies like lost items or reporting theft)

4. Medical Facilities

While Tokyo has excellent medical care, knowing where the nearest hospital is can save you time in an emergency. Here are a couple of reputable hospitals:

- **St. Luke's International Hospital** Address: 9-1 Akashi-cho, Chuo-ku, Tokyo Phone: +81 3-3541-5151 Website: https://www.luke.or.jp/english/
- **Keio University Hospital** Address: 35 Shinanomachi, Shinjuku City, Tokyo Phone: +81 3-3353-1211 Website: https://www.keio.ac.jp/en/

5. Local Apps and Services for Safety

In addition to traditional emergency services, you can use the following apps for real-time safety information or assistance while in Tokyo:

- **Japan Travel App (by NAVITIME)**: Provides up-to-date information on transportation, including routes, schedules, and possible disruptions.

- **Tokyo Metro App**: Offers subway maps, train schedules, and important notices about train services.
- **SOS Tokyo**: A helpful app for foreign visitors that includes emergency contact numbers and locations of essential services.

Final Thoughts

Tokyo is an incredibly safe city to visit, but it's always wise to be prepared for emergencies and to stay vigilant in crowded areas. By taking simple precautions, such as protecting your belongings, staying connected, and knowing the emergency contact information, you can ensure a smooth and enjoyable trip. If anything unexpected happens, remember that the local people are friendly and always willing to help, and you'll have the resources and knowledge to handle the situation with ease.

NIGHTLIFE IN TOKYO

Tokyo is a city that truly comes alive after the sun sets. Whether you're a night owl seeking vibrant nightlife or simply want to enjoy a quiet drink with a view, Tokyo has it all. From swanky rooftop bars to intimate jazz lounges and high-energy dance clubs, the options are as diverse as the city itself. In this section, you'll discover the best venues to experience Tokyo's nightlife, as well as the neighborhoods that pulse with energy well into the night. So, whether you're planning a night out with friends or a romantic evening with a loved one, Tokyo offers a nightlife experience like no other.

Popular Venues

Tokyo's nightlife is incredibly diverse, offering something for every taste. From cozy bars with live jazz to vibrant nightclubs pulsating with DJs, here are some of the most popular spots you can check out:

1. **Womb (Shibuya)**
   - **Type of Entertainment**: Womb is one of the most renowned nightclubs in Tokyo, offering a full clubbing experience with world-class DJs, vibrant light shows, and an international crowd. If you're into electronic music, this is the place to be.
   - **Entry Fees**: ¥3,000-¥5,000 depending on the night and DJ lineup. Special event nights might cost more.
   - **Additional Features**: The venue has an amazing sound system and spacious dance floors. VIP and bottle service are available.
   - **Contact/Website**: Womb Tokyo
2. **The New York Grill (Park Hyatt Tokyo, Shinjuku)**
   - **Type of Entertainment**: A stylish, upscale bar with panoramic views of Tokyo, this venue offers jazz performances and an intimate,

elegant atmosphere. Perfect for a cocktail with a view.

- Entry Fees: No entry fee, but drinks and meals can be expensive. Expect cocktails to cost between ¥1,200 and ¥2,500.
- Additional Features: Stunning skyline views, excellent service, and live jazz performances.
- Contact/Website: The New York Grill

3. Golden Gai (Shinjuku)
- Type of Entertainment: A unique area of tiny bars, each with its own theme and vibe. Golden Gai is great for hopping between different spots and experiencing Tokyo's old-school bar culture.
- Entry Fees: Most bars have a cover charge of ¥500-¥1,000. Drinks are usually ¥600-¥1,200.
- Additional Features: These intimate bars often offer a chance to chat with the bartender or locals. Each bar has its own distinctive decor and atmosphere.
- Contact/Website: Golden Gai doesn't have a central website due to the nature of its bars, but you can find more details and reviews on Golden Gai on Google Maps.

4. The Agave (Roppongi)
- Type of Entertainment: A sophisticated tequila and mezcal bar specializing in high-end agave spirits. They offer a variety of rare drinks and tasting experiences, paired with a classy, laid-back atmosphere.

- Entry Fees: Typically, no cover charge. Drink prices range from ¥1,000 to ¥3,000 depending on the selection.
- Additional Features: Expert bartenders who can educate you about the tequila and mezcal experience. Private tasting sessions available.
- Contact/Website: The Agave

5. Odeon Tokyo (Shibuya)
   - Type of Entertainment: A cozy bar and restaurant offering a laid-back vibe with great cocktails, wine, and an art-focused atmosphere. There are occasional live performances, too.
   - Entry Fees: No cover charge. Drinks are typically ¥800 to ¥1,500.
   - Additional Features: Ideal for a more relaxed evening with excellent cocktails and occasional live music.
   - Contact/Website: Odeon Tokyo doesn't have a dedicated website, but you can find more details on Google.

6. Bar Quest (Roppongi)
   - Type of Entertainment: A stylish and cozy jazz bar that features live performances every night. Ideal for a relaxing night out with classic cocktails and smooth tunes.
   - Entry Fees: No cover charge, but drinks range from ¥1,000 to ¥2,500.
   - Additional Features: Excellent selection of whiskey and cocktails, with a calm ambiance

perfect for couples or solo visitors looking to unwind.
- ○ **Contact/Website**: Bar Quest doesn't have a website, but it's listed on various local guides and review sites. You can check out reviews on Google.

7. **Ageha (Shinkiba)**
   - ○ **Type of Entertainment**: A massive nightclub known for its large-scale electronic music events. It features international DJs, a great sound system, and multiple dance floors.
   - ○ **Entry Fees**: Around ¥3,000-¥4,000 for regular nights, but special events can cost ¥5,000 or more.
   - ○ **Additional Features**: Open-air terrace, pool, and a very large dance space with impressive visuals and lighting.
   - ○ **Contact/Website**: Ageha

8. **JBS (Shibuya)**
   - ○ **Type of Entertainment**: One of the top jazz bars in Tokyo, JBS has a rich history and offers amazing live jazz performances in a classic setting.
   - ○ **Entry Fees**: No cover charge, but drinks typically cost between ¥1,000 and ¥2,000.
   - ○ **Additional Features**: Great for jazz lovers, JBS has live performances nightly and an intimate atmosphere.
   - ○ **Contact/Website**: JBS Tokyo

Best Neighborhoods for Nightlife Activities

Tokyo's nightlife is spread across a few key neighborhoods, each offering its own unique vibe and range of options. Here are the top areas to experience the city's after-dark scene:

1. Shibuya

- **Atmosphere**: Shibuya is known for its youthful energy and bustling streets. It's a hub for trendy clubs, bars, and late-night hangouts, attracting a mix of locals and tourists alike.
- **Types of Venues**: From the high-energy Womb nightclub to intimate bars and karaoke joints, Shibuya has something for every taste. Expect to find lively pubs, chic lounges, and large clubs with international DJs.
- **Convenience**: Shibuya is easily accessible by train, with several metro and JR lines passing through the area. You can walk or take a short taxi ride between the venues. It's also well-connected to other nightlife spots, making it a convenient base for exploring Tokyo at night.

2. Roppongi

- **Atmosphere**: Roppongi is known for its international crowd and upscale vibe. It's a popular nightlife district, especially for those looking for a more glamorous, sophisticated experience.

- **Types of Venues**: From upscale bars with panoramic views to nightclubs with top-tier DJs, Roppongi offers a refined, cosmopolitan feel. The area also boasts a selection of high-end lounges, restaurants, and karaoke bars.
- **Convenience**: Roppongi is served by the Tokyo Metro, and it's easy to reach by cab from other central locations. It's a safe area to explore at night, but as a popular tourist destination, it's always good to stay aware of your surroundings.

3. Shinjuku

- **Atmosphere**: Shinjuku is a blend of old-school Tokyo and modern energy. It's home to vibrant nightlife spots, ranging from classic izakayas to cutting-edge karaoke joints and exclusive cocktail bars.
- **Types of Venues**: Whether you're looking for traditional drinks at a cozy bar or a lively club experience, Shinjuku offers both. Omoide Yokocho (Memory Lane) offers a nostalgic dive into post-war Tokyo, while Kabukicho is known for its neon-lit streets and entertainment.
- **Convenience**: Shinjuku is a major transportation hub, with multiple train and metro lines connecting it to the rest of the city. It's an ideal spot for nightlife, offering plenty of late-night options to enjoy, and it's safe to walk around even in the early hours.

4. Akihabara

- **Atmosphere**: Akihabara's nightlife leans more toward the quirky, nerdy side, with anime-themed cafés, video game arcades, and maid cafés that offer an entirely different experience from the other districts.
- **Types of Venues**: Anime and manga enthusiasts will find plenty to do here, including themed cafés, bars, and gaming lounges. It's also a great area to explore if you're into virtual reality experiences, arcade games, or immersive tech-driven entertainment.
- **Convenience**: Akihabara is easy to navigate by metro, with direct lines from key central stations. The area is known for its bright lights and fun atmosphere, perfect for an unconventional nightlife experience.

5. Odaiba

- **Atmosphere**: Odaiba offers a more laid-back and scenic nightlife experience, with waterfront bars, restaurants, and attractions. It's perfect for a relaxed evening or a romantic night out.
- **Types of Venues**: No matter what type of nightlife experience you're seeking, Tokyo has a venue, neighborhood, and vibe that will suit your mood. Whether you're hopping between quirky bars in Golden Gai, dancing the night away in Roppongi's upscale nightclubs, or enjoying a quiet drink with a panoramic view at the Park Hyatt's New York Grill, the options are endless. Tokyo's nightlife is as dynamic as the city itself—always evolving, always surprising.

One thing is for sure: there's no better way to cap off a day of sightseeing than with a night out in one of the world's most exciting cities. As you explore these neighborhoods and venues, remember to stay safe, plan your transport ahead of time, and, most importantly, enjoy the experience. With Tokyo's world-class venues and diverse nightlife scene, you're bound to have an unforgettable night.

A Few Tips for Navigating Tokyo's Nightlife:

- **Transportation**: Public transport in Tokyo typically shuts down around midnight, so be sure to plan your ride home in advance. If you're out late, taxis or ride-sharing services are convenient, but they can be pricey. Alternatively, some nightlife districts like Shinjuku and Roppongi are walkable, so keep your hotel or accommodations in mind.
- **Dress Code**: While Tokyo nightlife is generally casual, some high-end clubs and bars may require a smart-casual dress code. It's a good idea to check before heading out, especially if you're planning to visit upscale venues like the New York Grill.
- **Etiquette**: When you visit clubs or bars, tipping is not expected in Tokyo. However, if you're enjoying a high-end experience or VIP service, a small gesture of appreciation can go a long way. Be polite and courteous to staff, and respect local customs, such as waiting in line at busy spots or not being too loud in more relaxed settings.

- **Late-Night Snacks**: After a night of drinking and dancing, head to one of Tokyo's many 24-hour ramen shops or conveyor-belt sushi joints. The late-night food scene is as delicious as it is varied, and grabbing a bite before heading back to your accommodation is a Tokyo tradition.

With the right mix of venues, neighborhoods, and tips in hand, you're all set to dive into Tokyo's vibrant nightlife. So, whether you're looking to unwind after a day of sightseeing or dance the night away, Tokyo's nightlife offers the perfect backdrop for your nighttime adventure. Enjoy every moment of Tokyo after dark, and create memories you'll cherish forever!

Currency and Money Matters in Tokyo

When traveling to Tokyo, it's essential to understand how to manage your money. Japan is a cash-based society, and while credit cards are increasingly accepted, you'll often find yourself using yen (JPY) in day-to-day transactions. This section will guide you through everything you need to know about currency, money exchange, and how to handle payments in Tokyo, ensuring you're financially prepared for your trip.

The Local Currency

Japan's official currency is the **yen** (¥), abbreviated as JPY. The yen is widely used throughout the country, and while it can sometimes feel a little overwhelming due to its variety of denominations, it's relatively straightforward once you become familiar with the notes and coins.

Banknotes

There are three main denominations of banknotes in Japan:

- **¥1,000** – The smallest banknote, often used for lower-priced goods or small purchases.
- **¥5,000** – A mid-range note, typically used for medium-range purchases or larger transactions.
- **¥10,000** – The largest banknote, often used for more significant expenses, such as shopping or hotel bills.

Japanese banknotes are relatively easy to distinguish due to their colors and the prominent historical figures printed on them. For example, the ¥1,000 note features the famous Japanese scientist Hideyo Noguchi, the ¥5,000 note features Ichiyo Higuchi, a literary figure, and the ¥10,000 note features Yukichi Fukuzawa, a renowned educator.

Coins

There are six denominations of coins in Japan:

- **¥1** – A small, light coin made of aluminum, used for very small purchases.
- **¥5** – A coin with a hole in the center, distinguished by its unique shape.
- **¥10** – A small bronze coin.

- **¥50** – A mid-sized coin with a hole in the center, made of brass.
- **¥100** – A silver-colored coin, similar in size to a US quarter.
- **¥500** – The largest coin, made of cupronickel, and often used for purchases like vending machines or small items.

Coins are used for smaller transactions, such as public transportation, vending machines, or street vendors. The ¥500 coin is often seen in larger transactions or tipping (though tipping is not customary in Japan).

Tips for Identifying Japanese Money

It may take some time to familiarize yourself with the yen, especially the various coins, as they can sometimes look quite similar. Here are a few tips to help you:

- **Color and Size**: Larger denominations of banknotes are darker and larger in size. The coins are also of varying sizes, with the ¥500 coin being the largest.
- **Feel and Shape**: Coins like the ¥5 and ¥50 have holes in the middle, which can make them easy to identify by touch.

Currency Exchange

Before you start spending yen, you'll need to exchange your home currency. Fortunately, there are plenty of options to exchange money in Tokyo.

Where to Exchange Currency

- **Airport Exchange Counters**: Most international airports, including Narita and Haneda, have currency exchange counters. However, the exchange rates at airports are typically not the best, and fees may be higher.
- **Currency Exchange Offices**: There are several dedicated exchange offices in central Tokyo, particularly in areas like Shinjuku, Shibuya, and Ginza. Look for *Travelex* or local exchanges for competitive rates.
- **Banks**: Banks are another reliable option for currency exchange, but they may have stricter hours, often opening only during weekdays. You'll need to bring your passport for verification.
- **ATMs**: Some ATMs in Tokyo allow you to withdraw yen using foreign debit or credit cards. Look for ATMs at convenience stores like **7-Eleven** or **Post Office ATMs**.

Getting the Best Exchange Rates

To get the best exchange rates, consider:

- **Avoiding Airport Exchange**: As mentioned, airport exchange counters tend to offer lower rates.
- **Using ATMs**: If your bank offers a good international withdrawal rate, ATMs may give you a better exchange rate than currency exchange counters.

- **Online Currency Exchange**: Some companies offer the option to pre-order yen online and pick up at the airport or a local office at a favorable exchange rate.

Foreign Currency Cards

Some travelers prefer to use prepaid foreign currency cards. These can be loaded with yen before you travel and used like a debit card at most locations in Tokyo. Some options include *Revolut*, *Wise*, or traditional travel money cards from your home bank. These cards often come with lower fees than withdrawing cash from international ATMs.

Using ATMs and Credit Cards

Japan has a robust ATM network, making it easy for travelers to access cash. However, there are some important things to keep in mind when using ATMs and credit cards.

Using ATMs in Tokyo

- **International ATMs**: Many **7-Eleven** convenience stores in Tokyo are equipped with ATMs that accept international cards. ATMs at **Japan Post Offices** also accept foreign cards. These machines allow you to withdraw yen with your international debit or credit card.
- **ATM Fees**: Be mindful of transaction fees. While Japan's ATMs are easy to use, your home bank may

charge an international withdrawal fee (usually a flat fee or a percentage of the withdrawal amount).

- **Hours of Operation**: ATMs in Japan are generally available 24/7 at convenience stores like 7-Eleven, but banks may have more limited hours, often closing around 5 or 6 pm.

Credit Cards in Tokyo

- **Widespread Acceptance in Urban Areas**: Tokyo has a high level of credit card acceptance, especially in hotels, department stores, restaurants, and larger shops. Visa, MasterCard, and American Express are the most commonly accepted cards.
- **Cash Preferred in Smaller Establishments**: Smaller shops, street vendors, taxis, and some traditional establishments may only accept cash. Always carry a sufficient amount of cash when exploring less touristy areas or using public transportation.
- **Notify Your Bank**: Before traveling, make sure to notify your bank that you'll be using your credit or debit card in Japan to avoid your card being blocked for security reasons.

Debit and Credit Card Fees

- **Foreign Transaction Fees**: Some credit cards charge a foreign transaction fee for international purchases. Be sure to check with your bank and consider getting a card that offers no foreign transaction fees.

- **Dynamic Currency Conversion**: Some merchants may offer to charge you in your home currency rather than yen, but this service often comes with poor exchange rates and additional fees. Always choose to be charged in yen.

Cash vs. Card

While credit cards are becoming more widely accepted in Japan, **cash is still king**. Many places, particularly smaller shops, local restaurants, and public transport systems, prefer cash transactions.

How Much Cash to Carry

- **Daily Budget**: It's a good idea to carry a mix of cash and a credit card, especially for situations where cash is essential. Aim to have around ¥5,000-¥10,000 in cash per day, depending on your planned activities.
- **Using ATMs for Cash**: Use ATMs at convenience stores (7-Eleven) or post offices to withdraw yen when needed. Always have some cash on hand for small purchases, taxis, or places that don't accept cards.

When to Use Cash

- **Public Transport**: While Tokyo's metro system accepts cards like Suica or PASMO for easy travel, some smaller stations or buses might require cash for tickets.

- **Temples and Markets**: Many traditional places, like shrines, temples, and markets, may only accept cash for donations, small goods, or souvenirs.
- **Taxis**: While some taxis in Tokyo accept credit cards, it's still common to pay in cash. Keep small bills on hand for convenience.

Tipping and Service Charges

In Japan, **tipping is not customary** and can even be considered rude. The Japanese value good service as part of their culture, and workers are not dependent on tips for their income.

- **Restaurants and Cafes**: There is no need to tip at restaurants or cafes. Service charges are not added to the bill either.
- **Taxis and Hotels**: Tipping taxi drivers or hotel staff is also not expected.
- **Service Charges**: In some high-end establishments, a service charge may be included in the bill, but tipping on top of this is not required.

Handling Money Safely

Japan is generally a safe country, but it's still important to be mindful of your money and valuables.

Money Safety Tips

- **Use Money Belts or Secure Bags**: Consider using a money belt or a crossbody bag with a secure zipper to protect your valuables.
- **Avoid Flashing Large Amounts of Cash**: While Tokyo is a very safe city, it's best to avoid pulling out large amounts of cash in crowded areas. Instead, use ATMs to withdraw smaller amounts as needed.

What to Do if You Lose Your Money or Cards

- **Lost Cash**: If you lose cash, unfortunately, there is no way to recover it. However, Tokyo's low crime rate means it's unlikely you'll be pickpocketed in the first place.
- **Lost Cards**: Immediately report a lost or stolen credit card to your card issuer. Contact your home country's embassy if necessary for any assistance with travel documents or emergency funds.

Language And Communication

Traveling to Tokyo can be an exciting and enriching experience, but language and communication may present a challenge for some visitors. While Japan's official language is Japanese, the good news is that Tokyo is a major international city, and there are plenty of ways to navigate language barriers. In this section, we'll provide you with the tools you need to communicate effectively, whether it's ordering food, asking for directions, or having a basic conversation. With a little preparation, you'll feel confident interacting with locals and making the most of your time in this fascinating city.

Language Overview

Tokyo, like the rest of Japan, primarily uses **Japanese** (日本語, *Nihongo*) as its official language. The majority of Tokyo residents speak Japanese as their first language, and it is the language of instruction in schools, business, and government.

While Japanese is the dominant language, **English** is becoming more commonly understood, especially in areas frequented by tourists. Many signs, menus, and information points in tourist-heavy areas such as Shinjuku, Shibuya, and Ginza have English translations. However, it's important to note that **English proficiency varies** widely among the population.

English in Tokyo

- **Younger Generations**: Many younger people in Tokyo, particularly those who work in the service and tourism industries, have learned basic English in school and may be able to help you with simple requests. English-speaking staff can also be found at larger hotels, restaurants, and shopping malls.
- **Older Generations**: Older Tokyoites, particularly those who are not involved in tourism, may have limited English proficiency. It's not uncommon to

encounter language barriers in smaller, more traditional shops or at less touristy locations.

While English is not universally spoken, you'll find that many locals are **patient and willing to help**, especially if you make an effort with a few words in Japanese.

Common Phrases and Greetings

Even if you don't speak Japanese fluently, learning a few key phrases can go a long way in making connections and showing respect for the local culture. Here are some essential phrases that will be useful during your trip:

Greetings and Polite Phrases

- **Hello** = こんにちは (*Konnichiwa*)
- **Good morning** = おはようございます (*Ohayou gozaimasu*)
- **Good evening** = こんばんは (*Konbanwa*)
- **Goodbye** = さようなら (*Sayounara*)
- **Thank you** = ありがとう (*Arigatou*) / **Thank you (very much)** = ありがとうございます (*Arigatou gozaimasu*)
- **Excuse me / I'm sorry** = すみません (*Sumimasen*)
- **Yes** = はい (*Hai*)
- **No** = いいえ (*Iie*)
- **How much is this?** = これはいくらですか？ (*Kore wa ikura desu ka?*)

- **Where is...?** = ...はどこですか？ (... *wa doko desu ka?*)
- **I don't understand** = わかりません (*Wakarimasen*)

Even using a few simple phrases like *sumimasen* (excuse me) or *arigatou* (thank you) will often be appreciated by locals. **Politeness** is highly valued in Japanese culture, so saying *arigatou gozaimasu* (thank you very much) adds an extra layer of respect to your interactions.

Using English in Tokyo

Tokyo is a **cosmopolitan city** where many establishments cater to tourists, so it's relatively easy to get by with English in some areas. However, in smaller or more local establishments, you might encounter communication difficulties. Here's what you should know about using English in Tokyo:

English in Tourist Areas

- **Tourist-Friendly Spots**: Most hotels, large department stores, and major restaurants in popular tourist areas will have **English-speaking staff** or at least an English menu available. Signs and information points at transportation hubs, like airports, train stations, and subway lines, are usually in both Japanese and English.
- **Menus and Signage**: You'll find many **English-language menus** in larger restaurants, cafes, and

shopping malls in districts like Shibuya, Ginza, and Akihabara. However, in smaller, family-run establishments or those outside tourist areas, **menus may only be in Japanese.**

In Smaller, Local Businesses

In smaller, local shops or traditional restaurants, communication may be more challenging, as English is not always spoken. If you encounter a language barrier, don't worry! Here are a few tips for dealing with situations where English isn't spoken:

- **Speak Slowly**: When speaking in English, slow down your speech and try to use simple, clear words.
- **Use Gestures**: Pointing or showing items can help clarify your needs. Japanese people often understand basic gestures or body language.
- **Use Translation Apps**: In case of a language barrier, translation apps (discussed below) can be a lifesaver.

Be Patient and Polite

It's important to approach communication with **patience.** Japanese people tend to be very polite, so if there's a misunderstanding, they will likely try to help you, even if it takes a little longer.

4. Translation Apps and Tools

In today's digital age, translation apps can be an invaluable tool for navigating language barriers in Tokyo. Here are some of the best apps you can use:

Google Translate

- **Google Translate** is one of the most popular translation apps. It offers translations between dozens of languages, including Japanese, and even has a **camera feature** that can translate text from photos or menus.
- It works offline as well, so you can download the Japanese language pack in advance if you'll be in areas without internet access.

Siri (Japanese Language)

- If you have an iPhone, Siri can be a useful tool for **basic translations**. By setting Siri to Japanese or asking in Japanese, you can get quick translations or assistance when you're on the go.

Offline Translation Tools

- If you don't have reliable internet access during your trip, consider downloading offline translation apps like **Microsoft Translator** or **iTranslate**. These apps can be incredibly useful in areas where you may not have a strong data connection.

5. Communication Etiquette

In Japan, **politeness** and **respect** are fundamental to communication. Here are a few cultural tips to help you interact respectfully with locals:

Politeness and Honorifics

- **Keigo**: Japanese has different levels of formality, called *keigo*, used in professional or respectful situations. While you don't need to master the intricacies of keigo as a visitor, using polite language (-*masu* form) will always be appreciated. For example, instead of just saying *arigatou*, say *arigatou gozaimasu* for extra respect.
- **Bowing**: Bowing is a traditional Japanese gesture that shows respect. While you don't need to bow deeply, a small bow (or just a nod) when greeting or thanking someone is a nice touch. In Tokyo, bowing is often done as a greeting or to show gratitude.

Polite Interactions

- **Avoiding Direct Confrontation**: In Japan, confrontation is generally avoided, and people tend to communicate indirectly, especially when discussing disagreement. Instead of saying "no" outright, the

Japanese might say *chotto* (a little) or use non-verbal cues to indicate hesitation.

- **Respectful Address**: When addressing others, it's polite to use honorifics like *san* after someone's name (e.g., *Takahashi-san*), especially in formal settings or when meeting someone for the first time.

6. Body Language and Non-Verbal Communication

Japanese culture places a strong emphasis on non-verbal communication. Here are some key things to keep in mind:

Personal Space and Touching

- **Personal Space**: Japanese people value personal space, especially in public places. Avoid standing too close to others, and avoid physical contact like handshakes, unless the situation calls for it.
- **Gestures**: In Japan, certain gestures, such as pointing or crossing your fingers, can have different meanings than in other cultures. It's best to avoid overly expressive gestures and maintain a calm, composed demeanor.

Shoes and Indoors

- **Removing Shoes**: In many traditional Japanese settings, such as homes, temples, and some restaurants, it's customary to remove your shoes before entering.

You will typically be provided with indoor slippers to wear once you remove your shoes.

Voice Levels

- **Keep Your Voice Low**: Japanese culture values quiet and polite behavior in public places. Avoid speaking too loudly, especially on public transportation. It's a good idea to keep your conversations in quieter tones, particularly in indoor spaces like cafes or libraries.

7. Signs and Menus

While **English signage** is commonly found in tourist areas, there may still be instances where you come across **Japanese-only signs or menus**. Here's what to do:

In Tourist Areas

In popular districts like Shibuya, Shinjuku, and Ginza, you'll find plenty of **English-language menus** and **bilingual signs**. Many restaurants, department stores, and major tourist attractions make an effort to cater to foreign visitors, offering English translations of important information.

In Smaller or Local Establishments

If you find yourself in a less touristy area or a traditional eatery, there may be only **Japanese signage or menus**. In these cases:

- **Learn Key Food Phrases**: Learning a few food-related phrases in Japanese, such as *osusume* (recommended) or *menu wa arimasu ka?* (Do you have a menu?), will help you navigate menus better.
- **Use Your Phone to Translate**: If no English menu is available, use a **translation app** to read the menu or ask your server about specific items.

8. Emergency Phrases

It's always wise to know some essential emergency phrases when traveling. Here are a few key phrases that could be useful in an emergency:

- **I need help** = 助けてください (*Tasukete kudasai*)
- **Call the police** = 警察を呼んでください (*Keisatsu o yonde kudasai*)
- **I'm lost** = 道に迷いました (*Michi ni mayoimashita*)
- **Where is the hospital?** = 病院はどこですか？ (*Byouin wa doko desu ka?*)

These phrases can help you handle basic emergencies and navigate situations where you need immediate assistance.

With a little effort and some basic knowledge of Japanese language and customs, you'll be able to communicate confidently and respectfully with locals in Tokyo. The Japanese are generally very friendly and patient, and most will appreciate your attempt to speak their language. Enjoy your travels and remember that communication is about making connections—language is just one tool to help you do so!

STAYING CONNECTED

Staying connected while traveling in Tokyo is essential for navigating the city, keeping in touch with loved ones, and accessing important services. Whether you need to stay on top of your itinerary, use maps to explore the city, or just want to send a quick message back home, Tokyo offers a variety of ways to stay connected. In this section, we'll guide you through the best options for internet access, mobile data, messaging services, and safety precautions to ensure that you can communicate effortlessly during your trip.

Internet Access in Tokyo

Japan is known for its high-speed internet, and Tokyo is no exception. The city boasts an extensive network of Wi-Fi hotspots and reliable internet access, ensuring that you can stay connected throughout your visit. Here's what you need to know:

Wi-Fi Availability

- **Public Wi-Fi**: Tokyo has a large number of public Wi-Fi hotspots, especially in popular tourist areas. Large shopping malls, airports, train stations, and cafes often offer free Wi-Fi for visitors. For example, you can find free Wi-Fi at locations like **Shibuya Station, Shinjuku Station,** and **Tokyo International Airport (Haneda)**. Some places may require you to **register** or input a **password** to connect, while others offer simple one-click access.

- **Hotels and Restaurants**: Most hotels, cafes, and restaurants in Tokyo offer free Wi-Fi, particularly in **tourist-friendly districts**. It's always a good idea to check with your accommodation beforehand to confirm Wi-Fi availability and whether any extra fees apply.

- **Wi-Fi in Public Spaces**: Many public parks and libraries also provide free Wi-Fi, but it's often limited in terms of speed and reliability. For these spaces, it's helpful to have a local SIM card or mobile hotspot as a backup.

Tips for Avoiding Excessive Roaming Fees

- **Wi-Fi at Accommodations**: Always confirm that your hotel or guesthouse offers free Wi-Fi during your stay. Many establishments will provide details about accessing Wi-Fi in the check-in process, or you can ask the front desk if unsure.

- **Use Wi-Fi Whenever Possible**: To avoid racking up expensive roaming charges, **connect to Wi-Fi whenever you can**. This will allow you to browse the web, use apps, and make calls via messaging apps (e.g., WhatsApp, LINE) without using up your mobile data.

SIM Cards and Mobile Data

If you prefer to stay connected on the go, purchasing a **local SIM card** for your phone is an easy and affordable option. Here's how you can get mobile data in Tokyo:

Where to Buy SIM Cards

- **Narita and Haneda Airports**: You can purchase SIM cards upon arrival at either of Tokyo's international airports. Both airports have counters for popular mobile providers where you can choose a short-term SIM card. Expect to pay around **¥2,000 to ¥5,000** for a **7-day SIM card** with 3GB to 5GB of data.
- **Convenience Stores and Mobile Shops**: In addition to the airports, **convenience stores** like 7-Eleven and Lawson often sell SIM cards, especially in the **Shibuya** or **Shinjuku** areas. Major **mobile carrier shops**, such as **SoftBank** or **Docomo**, also offer short-term data plans.

Popular SIM Card Providers

- **SoftBank**: Offers a variety of short-term SIM cards, including **unlimited data** for a set period (e.g., 7 or 30 days). Prices start around **¥2,500** for a 7-day plan with 2GB.
- **Docomo**: Known for reliable coverage, Docomo's prepaid SIM cards offer data-only plans or voice/data

bundles. Their 30-day plan (3GB) is priced around ¥3,000.

- **Rakuten Mobile**: Offers competitive pricing for SIM cards, with plans starting from ¥1,500 for basic data access. They also offer **free SIM card delivery** to your accommodation.

Renting a Pocket Wi-Fi (Mobile Hotspot)

If you need to stay connected with multiple devices (e.g., phone, tablet, laptop), renting a **pocket Wi-Fi** (mobile hotspot) is a convenient option. These small devices allow you to share internet access with several devices at once.

- Rental prices typically range from **¥500 to ¥1,000 per day** for unlimited data, and the rental process is simple. You can pick one up at the airport, or have it delivered to your accommodation.

Popular rental services include:

- **Japan Wireless**
- **SoftBank Global Rental**
- **Global Wi-Fi**

Required Documents

When purchasing a SIM card, you'll usually need to present a valid passport, as **registration is required** for each SIM card purchase under Japanese law.

Mobile Roaming Options

If you prefer to keep using your existing mobile provider while in Tokyo, **international roaming** might be a good option. However, this can be expensive, so it's essential to check your plan before you travel.

Check with Your Home Carrier

- **Roaming Charges**: Contact your carrier ahead of time to inquire about **roaming charges** and data plans for Japan. Some carriers offer **international plans** that can significantly reduce the cost of data usage abroad.
- **Network Compatibility**: Ensure that your phone is **unlocked** and compatible with Japanese networks. Japan uses **LTE/4G networks**, and while many phones will work, older models or phones locked to specific carriers may not.

Enable Roaming

Once you arrive in Tokyo, you may need to enable **data roaming** on your phone. Make sure to check your device's settings and confirm that roaming is turned on. If using mobile data is essential, consider switching off **data roaming** when you're near a free Wi-Fi hotspot.

Public Wi-Fi and Apps

Once you're connected to the internet, there are a few apps and tools that will make your time in Tokyo easier and more enjoyable. However, keep in mind that while public Wi-Fi is convenient, it's important to use it **securely**.

Public Wi-Fi Safety

- **Use VPNs**: When using public Wi-Fi, especially in areas like airports or cafes, it's important to stay safe. **VPNs** (Virtual Private Networks) provide an extra layer of security by encrypting your connection and preventing hackers from accessing your personal data.
- **Be Cautious**: Avoid using **banking apps** or entering sensitive information while connected to public Wi-Fi, as these networks can be less secure.

Using Messaging Services

Communication is essential when traveling, and **messaging apps** are incredibly popular in Japan. Here's what you need to know:

LINE – The Popular Messaging App

- **LINE** is Japan's most widely used messaging app, both for texting and calling. It's used by locals to chat with friends, family, and businesses, and it's perfect for staying in touch with anyone you meet during your trip.

- **Setting Up LINE**: You can download LINE for free from the App Store or Google Play. Once set up, you can send messages, make free voice or video calls, and share photos and stickers.

WhatsApp and Facebook Messenger

- For international communication, apps like **WhatsApp** or **Facebook Messenger** work well if you have internet access through Wi-Fi or mobile data. Just make sure you're connected to avoid additional charges.

Paying for Data or Wi-Fi Access

Staying connected on your trip means understanding how to pay for mobile data or Wi-Fi access. Here's a breakdown of your options:

Public Wi-Fi:

- Many public Wi-Fi networks are free in Tokyo, but some locations (like cafes or hotels) may require you to pay for access, especially if you're staying for extended periods. **Hourly or daily fees** typically range from **¥300 to ¥1,000**.

SIM Card & Pocket Wi-Fi Rentals:

- As mentioned earlier, SIM cards and pocket Wi-Fi rentals can be paid for upfront. Prices for **SIM cards** vary based on the data package, and pocket Wi-Fi rentals are usually **paid daily**.

Budgeting for Connectivity:

- Depending on your connectivity needs, you should budget about **¥3,000 to ¥5,000 per week** for mobile data or Wi-Fi access. If you're mainly using free Wi-Fi, this can be a cost-effective way to stay connected.

Staying Safe and Secure Online

While staying connected is essential, online security should always be a priority. Here are some tips to keep your information safe:

Avoid Public Wi-Fi for Sensitive Transactions

- Avoid accessing **personal banking accounts** or **making purchases** while connected to public Wi-Fi. Use a VPN if you must access sensitive information.

Enable Two-Factor Authentication

- For added security, enable **two-factor authentication** for your email and banking accounts. This adds an extra layer of protection to your sensitive information.

Secure Your Devices

- Always **lock your phone** with a PIN, password, or biometric security feature like fingerprint or face recognition to protect your personal data.

Emergency Communication

In the unlikely event of an emergency, staying connected can be crucial. Here are a few tips:

- **Keep Important Numbers**: Store important phone numbers in your device (e.g., embassy, hotel, emergency contacts).
- **Emergency Contact Apps**: Consider downloading apps like **ICE (In Case of Emergency)** or **Safety Tips** to have easy access to emergency information.
- **Report Lost or Stolen Devices**: If your phone is lost or stolen, immediately contact your mobile provider to report it and deactivate your SIM card.

With the right tools and knowledge, staying connected while traveling in Tokyo is easy and secure. Whether you're using a SIM card, relying on Wi-Fi hotspots, or renting a mobile hotspot, you'll have plenty of options to stay in touch with the world and access all the essential services you need.

CONCLUSION

Tokyo is a city of contrasts—where centuries-old traditions meet futuristic innovation, where serene gardens coexist with bustling streets, and where every corner offers a new adventure. From exploring the grandeur of historic temples and shrines to diving into the energy of neon-lit districts, Tokyo offers a rich tapestry of experiences that will stay with you long after your trip ends.

Whether you're savoring world-class sushi at a hidden gem or enjoying the breathtaking views from a rooftop bar, Tokyo's dining scene, vibrant nightlife, and cultural landmarks will leave you with memories to cherish. If you seek peaceful moments, Tokyo's beautiful parks, tranquil temples, and stunning gardens provide the perfect escape. For the more adventurous, the city's endless entertainment options—from quirky themed cafes to dynamic shopping streets—ensure that boredom is never an option.

Now that you have all the tools and tips you need, it's time to start planning your adventure. This guide is here to help you make the most of every moment in Tokyo, whether you're a first-time visitor or returning to explore the city in a new light. You've learned where to go, what to do, and how to navigate the cultural nuances that will make your experience even richer.

There's no better time than now to turn your dream trip to Tokyo into a reality. From iconic landmarks to hidden gems, there's always something new to discover in this incredible city. So pack your bags, get ready to embark on a journey of a lifetime, and prepare for the unforgettable memories waiting for you in Tokyo. Every moment is an opportunity to explore, connect, and immerse yourself in a city like no other.

Made in the USA
Coppell, TX
22 January 2025

44793074R00095